Smart Persuasion

arketers
ısumers
Take Action)

Philippe AIMÉ &
Jochen GRÜNBECK

INCLUDED
Actionable Tactics
for each principle

Smart Persuasion

by Philippe AIMÉ & Jochen GRÜNBECK

Copyright © 2019 Convertize Ltd

First published March 2019 in the United Kingdom

Copyright Information:

All rights reserved. No part of this publication may be reproduced, distributed, or transmitted in any form or by any means, including photocopying, recording, or other electronic or mechanical methods, without the prior written permission of the publisher, except in the case of brief quotations embodied in critical reviews and certain other non-commercial uses permitted by copyright law.

Some images have been taken from Freepik (www.freepik.com).

For permission requests, write to the Permissions Coordinator at the address below:

Philippe AIMÉ
Convertize Ltd
12 Hammersmith Grove,
London, W6 7AP
United Kingdom

press@convertize.com
www.convertize.com

ISBN: 9781798004180

Contents

Acknowledgements vii

Foreword ix

How to use this book xv

How priming and framing can influence your visitors and guide their behaviour

PRINCIPLE	PAGE
1 Decoy Effect	3
2 Hobson's +1 Choice Effect	7
3 Anchoring Effect	11
4 Framing Effect	15
5 Loss Aversion	19
6 Choice Closure	23
7 Psychology of Consumption	25
8 Reference Pricing	29
9 Zeigarnik Effect	33
10 Single-Option Aversion	37
11 Mere-Exposure Effect	41
12 Serial Position Effect	45
13 Focusing Effect	49
14 Partitioned Pricing	53
15 Default Effect	57
16 Magnitude Encoding Process	61
17 Time vs Money Effect	65
18 Recency Effect	67
19 Cheerleader Effect	69

How to address intrinsic and extrinsic needs and motivate your visitors to act

20 Self-Efficacy Theory 75
21 Need for Certainty 79
22 Ben Franklin Effect 83
23 Cognitive Ease 87
24 Curse of Knowledge 91
25 Ambiguity Effect 95
26 Extrinsic Motivation 99
27 Cognitive Friction 103
28 Motivating Uncertainty Effect 107
29 Choice-Supportive Bias 111
30 Paradox of Choice 115
31 Foot-in-the-door Technique (FITD) 119
32 Intention and Self-Regulation 123
33 Autonomy Bias 127
34 Having vs Using Effect 129
35 Scarcity 133
36 Commitment and Consistency 135
37 Metaphor Effect 137
38 Psychological Reactance 141
39 Immediacy Effect 143
40 Information Bias 147
41 Pain of Paying 149
42 Sunk Cost Effect 153
43 Reciprocity Principle 157
44 Fear of Missing Out (FOMO) 161
45 Illusion of Control 165

How to capture your visitors' attention and make your offers more persuasive

46 Von Restorff Effect 171
47 Gaze Cueing 173
48 Visual Cueing 175
49 Risk Compensation 177
50 Zero-Risk Bias 179
51 Attention Ratio 183
52 Aesthetic Usability Effect 185
53 Contrast Principle 187
54 Weber's Law 191
55 Cognitive Dissonance 193
56 Processing Efficacy 197
57 Endowment Effect 201
58 Split-Attention Effect 203
59 Perceived Value Pricing 207
60 Centre-Stage Effect 211
61 Salience Effect 215
62 Representativeness Heuristic 219
63 Picture Superiority Effect 221
64 Visual Depiction Effect 223
65 Physical Attractiveness 225
66 Halo Effect 229
67 Base Rate Fallacy 233

How social biases affect your customers, and what you can do with them

68 In-Group Bias 237
69 Social Proof 239
70 Authority Principle 243
71 Social Comparison Theory 247
72 Social Cognition 249

Conclusion 251

ACKNOWLEDGEMENTS

We say **thank you**.

Because this book wouldn't exist without many of you.

Thank you to some of the greatest minds of the past decades who are still inspiring us to move forward and learn. As Nelson Mandela put it: "*I never lose, I either win or learn.*"

Thank you to some of the finest academics, researchers, authors and practitioners in the fields of behavioural economics, neuroscience, persuasion science and consumer psychology. It would require an entire chapter to list them all, so here are just a few of them:

Dan Ariely, Daniel Kahneman, Richard Thaler, Amos Tversky, George Loewenstein, Robert Cialdini, Noah Goldstein, Steve Martin, Richard Wiseman and Nick Kolenda.

A few **specific thanks** (in no particular order) to:

Benjamin Ligier, Ben Robertson & Stephen Courtney, for helping to aggregate the extensive research in this book.

Aleksander Góra, for his vision and execution of the layout and design of this book as well as the underlying technology.

Syed Sami, for his countless hours in designing the book and producing hundreds of illustrations.

Ernestas Staugaitis, for his dedicated work in creating our online database of Persuasion principles.

Matt Green & Nora Popova, for tireless proofreading and reference-checking.

Thank you to our clients. They help us grow by questioning our thinking and contributing their wisdom.

Thank you to those who helped us learn through their hands-on experience: **Jonah Berger, Roger Dooley, John Ekman, Oli Gardner, Chris Goward, Peep Laja, Brian Masséy, Andre Morys, Neil Patel, Bart Schutz, Ton Wesseling** and many more.

Thank you to the conference organisers and business leaders who have invited us to speak to their audiences.

Thanks to our amazing team, without whom this book would not have been possible. Everybody from Convertize contributed to building this book: Some by creating new bricks, some by inventing a new sort of mortar, and some by making sure that the builders always had freshly-brewed espresso close by!

And last, but not least, we say thank you to the reader, for deciding to read this book.

Foreword

Foreword

Have you ever wondered why some websites stand out when it comes to turning visitors into customers?

According to a recent study, members of Amazon Prime convert on a remarkable 74% of their sessions...

...and Booking.com's conversion rates are one of their best-kept secrets.

Would you believe that much of their success is rooted in the work of a number of psychologists, behavioural economists and even Nobel Prize winners?

Sometimes, this research dates back a long way. For example, our understanding of the Von Restorff Effect can be traced to a warm summer day in Berlin, 1933. It was here that Hedwig von Restorff, who completed her Ph.D. in psychology at the tender age of 27, submitted the results of her research to the then famous Gestalt journal *Psychologische Forschung*.

She could not have known at the time that her research was going to revolutionize marketing throughout the 20th century. Nor could she have guessed that it would help to shape new forms of commerce in the 21st century.

Today, thanks to her research:

- You can make sure readers remember your brand
- You can increase the click-through rate on an ad or banner by up to 230%
- You can pull your readers' attention to a Call To Action button as if it is magnetic

Other times, this research is quite modern. On an otherwise normal Friday afternoon in 1985, Dan Ariely was exposed to the flame of a magnesium flare (usually used to light battlefields). At the age of 18, he suffered 3rd degree burns on 70% of his body. The situations he encountered during an agonising recovery, in particular the way his nurses attempted to reduce the suffering caused by painful procedures, inspired him to study the origins of human behaviour. Ariely is now one of the most renowned writers and researchers in behavioural economics.

His work helps us understand why we would rather buy a bigger and more expensive cappuccino than a small one:

Ariely encountered a similar situation whilst teaching a class of students at MIT. He came across the following offers in an online ad by *The Economist*:

- Online-only subscription $59 USD / year
- Print-only subscription $125 USD / year
- Print & online subscription $125 USD / year

Who would ever buy the print-only subscription for the same price as the print AND online subscription? Indeed, in a number of experiments conducted on his unsuspecting students, Ariely found that none of his subjects chose the print-only subscription. Despite this, eliminating the option had an unexpected effect on their choices.

When the print-only option was removed, more students chose the cheaper online-only offer and the revenue produced fell by 30%. Ariely's case study demonstrated an important principle that has since been reproduced in countless forms: Decoy Pricing.

Then there is Daniel Kahneman, who received the 2002 Nobel Prize in Economics: the first psychologist to win in that category. Kahneman described the two modes of thinking we use when dealing with different problems: the "Fast" one (System

1) and the "Slow" one (System 2). It is thanks to his work that we know the most important advice for designing a website that visitors will appreciate: **"Don't make them think!"**

Thanks to Kahneman, we know that the perceived pain from losing $100 is roughly twice as strong as the perceived joy of winning $100. What's more, we know how to use this knowledge to improve conversion rates.

There are many other effects that can't be explained with rational models of economics or consumer behaviour. For example:

- Why do the majority of us prefer $50 today instead of $100 in one year?
- Why should you first ask for something small before asking for something bigger?
- Why can too much choice kill your sales, and what should you do instead?

Smart online marketers know to apply these principles to make their website more persuasive.

This book would not exist if it wasn't for the work of people like Hedwig von Restorff, Dan Ariely and Daniel Kahneman. We are indebted to these people and to a great number of other psychologists and behavioural economists, including Amos Tversky, George Lowenstein, Robert Cialdini and Noah Goldstein, to name a few.

Their research has contributed to the success of eCommerce giants such as Amazon. It is thanks to them that even the tiniest hotel in the Chilean desert is ready to pay a whopping 15% of its revenue to Booking.com (and some of the best-known establishments in Paris, London or Rome fork out 25% or more).

Philippe and I took the time to aggregate this research, distilling its principles and producing a collection of proven psychological effects.

Like me, Philippe is obsessed with optimisation. He also has the humility to recognize that, as an expert, you need to learn and to "unlearn" all the time. In a world where everything changes every 3 months (or, even, every 3 weeks) experts should always be ready to question what they believed yesterday.

But, whilst traffic acquisition and social media strategies seem to change from day to day, psychological principles such as reciprocity, salience, motivation or aversion, have been proven to work since the moment they were discovered.

In this book, we will show you how to apply these concepts to increase conversions time and time again. We guarantee that you will soon be converting more of your website visitors into customers.

Jochen Grünbeck (Insead MBA)
Associate Director at Convertize
March 2019

How to use this book

How to use this book

First, let's talk about structure. The 72 persuasion principles listed at the start of this book have been split into four categories:

Category 1: Priming and Framing

How priming and framing can influence your visitors and guide their behaviour

Category 2: Needs and Motivation

How to address intrinsic and extrinsic needs and motivate your visitors to act

Category 3: Attention and Perception

How to capture your visitors' attention and make your offers more persuasive

Category 4: Social Biases

How social biases affect your customers, and what you can do with them

Why these categories?

These are the four categories into which any cognitive bias can be grouped. Cognitive biases, the mental shortcuts that shape our decisions without us realising, can lead us to think and behave in irrational ways. They are responsible for all of the persuasion principles described in this book.

Some of the principles we describe can be placed in more than one group. For example, "Scarcity" is included in the category "Needs and Motivation" because it increases the motivation to act. But it is also a framing technique and could therefore be included in "Priming and Framing".

When there was a doubt about which category to place a principle in, we made a decision based on the original scientific studies.

Each principle has been presented in such a way that a reader can quickly understand and apply it. The chapters are comprised of five sections:

- Description of the principle
- Why this principle works
- How to use this principle
- Concrete application example
- Sources and further reading

We have also provided references to the research that each principle is based on. That way, you can explore the studies and experiments that have inspired us.

Priming and Framing

How priming and framing can influence your visitors and guide their behaviour

> Principle 1

Decoy Effect

(Huber, Payne & Puto, 1982; Dan Ariely, 2008)

Description of the Principle:

The Decoy Effect, first demonstrated in 1982 by Joel Huber at Duke University, explains how, when a customer is hesitating between two options, presenting them with a third "asymmetrically dominated" option (acting as a decoy) will strongly influence their choice. An option can be defined as asymmetrically dominated when it is completely dominated by (i. e. definitely inferior to) one option and only partially dominated (i. e. inferior in some aspects) by the other. The asymmetrically dominated option serves as a decoy which increases preference for the dominating option – the one we really want the consumer to choose.

For example, imagine you own a café and you sell two sizes of your coffee. A small cup costs $1.20, whilst a large costs $2.50. Whilst the large cup provides more coffee, it is also markedly more expensive.

The Decoy Effect will come into play if you introduce a third option. If you introduce a medium coffee and price it at $2.20, it will serve as a decoy. This option is partially inferior to a small coffee, as it is bigger but a whole $1 more expensive. However it is completely inferior to the large coffee, which provides more coffee and is only marginally more expensive. With these comparisons in mind, the large coffee will stand out as being the best value.

Why this Principle works:

This cognitive bias takes place because our brains prefer to evaluate things based on comparative, rather than absolute, values. When a customer has to choose between just two products, it can make for a difficult decision. In the aforementioned example, the two initial options have nothing in common in terms of price or size, which makes it difficult to draw an effective comparison. The customer can't clearly see which is the "better" choice because they offer totally different benefits: one has a good price, but the other provides more coffee. By introducing the third option, a more relevant point of comparison is offered (even if it is distorted in order to sway the decision making process a certain way). The fact that the third option offers much less coffee for a comparatively small difference in price suddenly makes the large coffee the outstanding option in terms of value for money.

How to use this Principle:

This theory has vast applications in sales and digital marketing, and can be applied to anything from pricing to determining the arrangement and grouping of products.

Concrete Application Example:

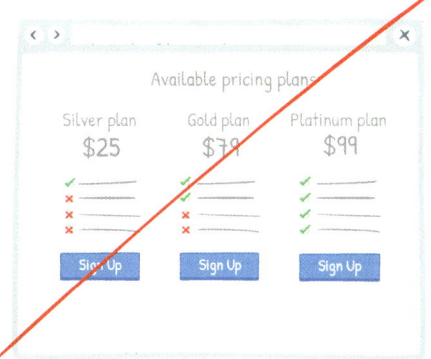 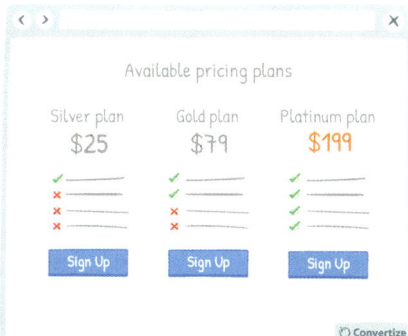

Displaying a pricing plan that is disproportionately expensive can be an effective decoy. Supposing you would like your customers to select a particular pricing plan ("Gold"), offering a third option ("Platinum") with similar features but a much higher cost will make your preferred plan seem like a better deal.

People will feel like they are getting better value for money because they are "saving" a lot in comparison to the more expensive third option (the decoy).

Sources and further examples:

Sources:
- Huber, Payne & Puto, 1982
- Dan Ariely, 2008

Further examples on this PRIVATE page:
- www.smart-persuasion.com/decoy-effect

Principle 2

Hobson's +1 Choice Effect

(Huber, Payne & Puto, 1982)

Description of the Principle:

To understand Hobson's +1 Choice Effect, you first need to know what a Hobson's choice is. A Hobson's choice is a situation that involves a single option which you can either accept or refuse. In other words, it's a "take it or leave it" choice. The expression comes from Thomas Hobson who was a wealthy landowner and stable owner in the 17th Century. Despite having a wide range of horses for people to ride, he would only allow his customers to take the horse that was nearest the stable door at the time. He did not want the best horses to get overworked by allowing people to choose for themselves. Hobson's customers could either take the horse nearest the stable door or not go riding at all; the choice was theirs.

Hobson's Choice has therefore become a widely-used expression for offering people a single option to either accept or refuse. Leading on from this, a Hobson's +1 Choice is when you offer somebody two options to choose from instead.

Why this Principle works:

Psychologist Barry Schwartz developed the concept of the Paradox of Choice in 2004, which shows how people become overwhelmed when they have too many options. However, Schwartz noticed that this effect only comes into play after 3 or more choices. In fact, it is usually better to offer people two options rather than only one. Research has shown that, when confronted with a true Hobson's Choice, we are more likely to go for the "leave it" than the "take it" option.

If a second alternative is added, we feel more inclined to opt for one of the choices offered to us. This cognitive bias can be explained as follows: when we are faced with a "take it or leave it" choice, we use all our mental energy deciding whether to buy a product or not to buy it. However, when we are given two options, we use the same mental energy to compare these offers instead of considering the "leave it" option. This makes it much more likely that at least one of the "active" choices will be made.

How to use this Principle:

Hobson's +1 Choice Effect has many applications in business and marketing in terms of the sales strategies used when proposing offers and products to your customers.

For example, in online sales, it is often best to give your customers the opportunity to choose between two options with your Call To Action buttons, rather than putting them in the position of "taking or leaving" just one option.

Concrete Application Example:

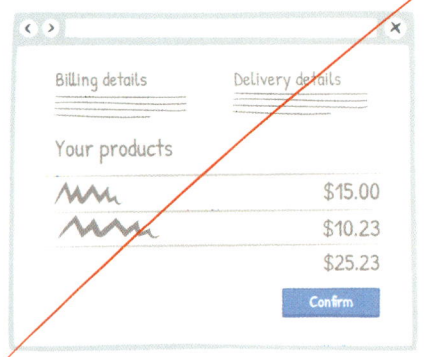 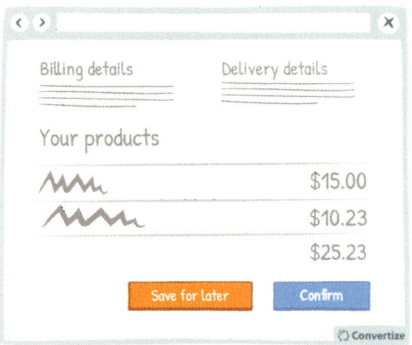

Your customers will appreciate having the choice between making their purchase immediately or saving their items in order to complete the purchase later.

People like to feel as though they are in control of their shopping experience, and giving them the option to save a basket for later will help to enhance their sense of autonomy. The more that a customer feels they are in control of the situation, the more positive they will feel about eventually making the purchase.

Sources and further examples:

Sources:
- Tversky & Kahneman, 1981
- Huber, Payne & Puto, 1982
- O'Keefe & Jensen, 2008

Further examples on this PRIVATE page:
www.smart-persuasion.com/hobsons-1-choice-effect

Principle 3

Anchoring Effect

(Tversky & Kahneman, 1974)

Description of the Principle:

The Anchoring Effect, first studied by Tversky & Kahneman (1974), is a cognitive bias that causes people to rely on the first piece of information they receive as a point of reference. The human mind does not consider the value of something based on its intrinsic value but rather compares multiple things, using these comparative values to make decisions. Anchoring occurs when an individual uses an initial reference point to make judgments about subsequent information.

Why this Principle works:

The Anchoring Effect influences our negotiations, the prices we consider to be acceptable and the value we attribute to things. Many experiments have shown that it is difficult to avoid the Anchoring Effect, as it affects our thinking even when we're aware of it. In one study, two groups of students were asked to guess at what age Mahatma Gandhi died. The first group were asked whether they thought he died before or after age 9, and the second group before or after age 140 (both anchors far removed from reality, as Gandhi actually died at 87 years old). The experiment showed that the two groups gave significantly different answers – of 50 and 67 respectively – precisely because they had been influenced by the anchoring values initially given.

How to use this Principle:

Numerous examples of the Anchoring Effect can be found in the commercial sector: during sales, it is common practice to show the original price crossed out with a sale price right below it. This gives customers the anchor point of the higher original price and makes the new one seem like a comparatively good deal.

Concrete Application Example:

Exposing website visitors to high numbers before displaying a product's price can be very effective in influencing their perception of the product's value.

Studies have shown that people use the first piece of information they receive as an anchoring point by which to judge subsequent information. Showing high numbers to your visitors will ensure that, by comparison, your prices seem lower than they otherwise would.

Any large number will work, with no link to pricing necessarily required. The anchor you provide could be based on the number of members you have, the number of satisfied customers, or the number of visitors you receive per month.

Sources and further examples:

Sources:
- Tversky & Kahneman, 1974; 1981
- O'Keefe & Jensen, 2008

Further examples on this PRIVATE page:
www.smart-persuasion.com/anchoring-effect

Framing Effect

(Tversky & Kahneman, 1981; O'Keefe & Jensen, 2008)

Description of the Principle:

The Framing Effect is a cognitive bias that explains how we react differently to things depending on how they are presented to us. Being aware of, and altering, the way information is presented can influence how it is received. Framing something in a certain way – through the use of images, words and context – will shape people's interpretations of it.

Why this Principle works:

Generally, positive framing will spur people into action and encourage possible risk-taking, whereas negative framing will lead people to inaction or the cessation of activity. Framing information negatively (loss-framed messaging) is widely used to try and scare people into better behaviour or into not doing something. The government and media use it regularly to shock us into not doing certain things: smoking, drink driving, voting for an opponent, etc..

It has widely been thought to be more motivating than positive framing because of the simple fact that it does shock and scare, meaning the message should stay with you for longer. However, recent studies conducted by O'Keefe & Jensen (2008) have shown that we actually react better to positive framing. Positive framing can lead to happier thoughts, more motivated actions and a greater synergy with the message provider.

We don't like to be chastised, bullied and told what we should or shouldn't do by governments. But perhaps if they highlighted all the positive outcomes of making a certain decision (for example, telling people how much healthier they would become if they gave up smoking, rather than concentrating on the horror of lung cancer) then they might receive a more positive reaction.

How to use this Principle:

In advertising and marketing especially, it is important to frame your messages in the correct way. Generally, it's better to use positive framing, as you want your brand to be associated with positive, motivational feelings that lead people to act (buy your product, give to your charity, subscribe to your newsletter). Framing your messages in a positive light – pointing out all the benefits that could be gained – should help to encourage people to buy into the lifestyle you're selling and also to give them positive thoughts associated with your brand. For example, in a study by Levin & Gaeth (1988), customers gave better reviews of ground beef labelled 75% lean than the same product labelled as 25% fat.

However, there may be instances where negative framing will have a better effect. For example, a charity seeking donations during a humanitarian crisis may get a better reaction from detailing all the horrors of the crisis than the benefits of a small donation. It is important to ensure that the framing is carefully tailored to the situation.

Concrete Application Example:

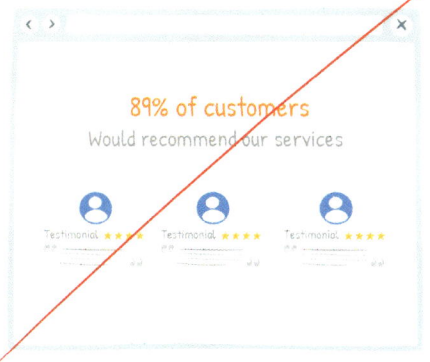 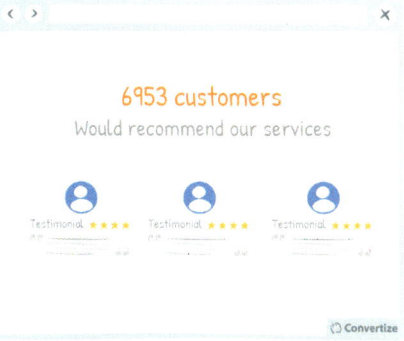

Your visitors will perceive the same information in different ways depending on how you present it to them. It is important, therefore, to ensure you present information using appropriate framing so that it is interpreted in the most positive way possible. When giving information related to people (number of members, subscribers, customers, etc.), using a percentage is quite impersonal and takes away from the effect of this information; it is preferable to reinforce the tangible human dimension by presenting your statistics in numbers instead.

Customers are more likely to connect and identify with the information when it is presented in this way. They will see the real individuals behind the statistic and attach an emotional human response to them, giving more weight to their opinions than they would to an abstract percentage.

Sources and further examples:

Sources:
- Tversky & Kahneman, 1981
- Levin, Schneider and Gaeth (1998)
- O'Keefe & Jensen, 2008

Further examples on this PRIVATE page:
www.smart-persuasion.com/framing-effect

Loss Aversion

(Tversky & Kahneman, 1979)

Description of the Principle:

Loss Aversion was first discussed by Amos Tversky and Daniel Kahneman in 1979. This principle refers to the fact that the negative emotions experienced when losing something are psychologically about twice as powerful as the positive emotions experienced from the pleasure of gaining something.

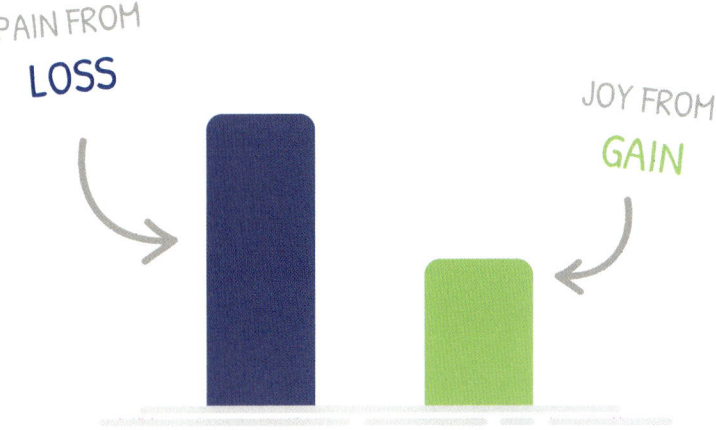

In other words, the idea of losing or giving something up provokes a stronger reaction in us than the possibility of gaining something. The avoidance of loss is therefore a strong motivator for us, and can lead us to act in certain, sometimes irrational, ways in order to avoid losing out on something.

Why this Principle works:

This desire to avoid the negative feelings associated with loss explains other cognitive biases that also influence our behaviour, such as the Sunk Cost Effect (Principle 42), which describes the way in which we prefer to continue on with something as a result of previously invested resources of time, money or effort, even if we are no longer satisfied with it. The Endowment Effect (Principle 57) is also closely linked. It explains the way in which we place higher value on something we already own than something that isn't in our possession.

One example of Loss Aversion we can all relate to is when you sit through the entirety of an awful movie in the cinema, simply because you've already paid for the ticket. After investing time and money, we feel we would be losing out if we left half-way through. In reality, that money has already gone and you won't be getting your time back either way, so the rational decision would be to leave and cut your losses. The pain of losing makes us act irrationally, as we would rather retain our initial investment than gain more pleasurable time. We make this biased decision because the brain is telling us that not losing out on something is better than gaining something.

How to Use this Principle:

Loss Aversion is utilised in sales and marketing to influence and motivate consumers' buying decisions. If you are able to make your customers feel as though they are going to "lose out" on an offer, this is likely to motivate them to complete their purchase. This strategy is often seen in online marketing through the use of motivational phrasing such as "offer not to be missed" or "only 2 rooms still left," etc.

Concrete Application Example:

Loss Aversion is the scientific term for the pain we feel when we lose something. It is about twice as powerful, psychologically, as the pleasure of gaining something.

In general, people will be more motivated to act if they think they are going to lose out on something than if they only concentrate on what they might gain.

Therefore, pointing out that your customer may miss out on a deal or lose out financially by shopping elsewhere will provoke the powerful emotions associated with Loss Aversion. They will then be more likely to make a purchase than if you merely point out what they will gain.

Sources and further examples:

Sources:
- Tversky & Kahneman, 1979; 1981
- O'Keefe & Jensen, 2008

Further examples on this PRIVATE page:
www.smart-persuasion.com/loss-aversion

Principle 6

Choice Closure

(Gu, Botti & Faro, 2013; Johnson, 2007)

Description of the Principle:

When we make decisions, we're often racked with post-decision regret, constantly wondering what life might have been like had we made a different one. Choice Closure explains how this can be avoided to a certain extent through the simple act of physical closure. Being able to complete a physical act of closure helps our brains to accept the finality of a choice, allowing the decision-maker to move on from alternate possibilities and be much more satisfied with their choice. As humans, we are more able to grasp abstract ideas through physical experiences (Johnson, 2007). Adding action and imagery to the concept of closure makes a decision feel more final. This physical act can be as simple as closing a menu or internet browser.

Why this Principle works:

Choice Closure can help to limit unfavourable afterthoughts about a choice we've made and to raise satisfaction with what we have chosen. Gu, Botti & Faro (2013) conducted an experiment at the London Business School whereby people were asked to choose from a range of 24 different tea varieties. It was made very clear to them that they wouldn't be able to alter their choice afterwards. Some people were asked to close their menu after they'd chosen and results overwhelmingly showed that these people were far more satisfied with their choice of tea than those who were simply asked to make a choice. The only difference was that one small act of closing the menu, which closed those participants' minds off to alternate choices and post-choice regrets.

How to use this Principle:

Choice Closure is a really useful tool in the commercial world, as it helps to improve customer satisfaction post-sale, which in turn leads to repeat business and future sales. Offering some kind of Choice Closure to customers is particularly beneficial when a large number of options have been available. Too many options can lead to the Paradox of Choice (Principle 30), whereby people struggle to make a decision and are more likely to regret their choices afterwards.

Concrete Application Example:

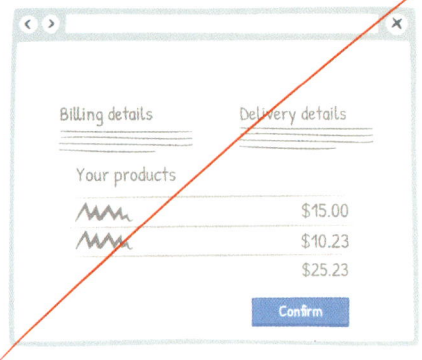
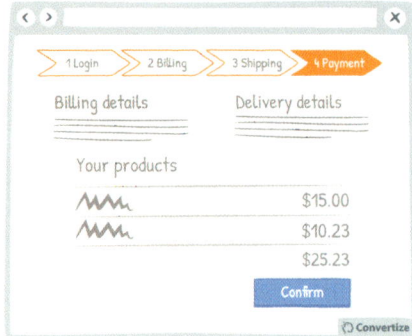

Displaying a progress bar is a great visual way to help users follow their progress in the purchase process and will not only stimulate their desire to continue to the end of the process, but also give an important sense of closure once it is completed.

People will become more invested and interested in a task if they can clearly see the steps they need to take before it is finished, and they will see movement along your progress bar as encouragement for completing their order. Having this sense of direction assists cognitive functioning. The visual closure at the end is proven to help customers feel more satisfied with the purchase they've made.

Sources and further examples:

Sources:
- Gu, Botti & Faro, 2013
- Johnson, 2007

Further examples on this PRIVATE page:
www.smart-persuasion.com/choice-closure

Principle 7

Psychology of Consumption

(Gourville, 2002)

Description of the Principle:

The Psychology of Consumption is a concept that looks past merely selling a product or service, to the importance of the post-purchase consumption rate for guaranteeing repeat purchases. With the high amount of competition for almost every product and service today, the key to long-term success is not only securing the initial purchase, but also ensuring people actually use the product and services they buy.

We often favour an unobtrusive payment process because it increases the likelihood of making a sale. However, this tactic has no effect on ensuring a customer actually uses that product to the extent that they become a returning customer. One of the most effective ways to ensure someone makes use of something they've bought is to consistently remind them of their investment. This is in line with the Sunk-Cost Effect (Principle 42), which describes how individuals will make sure they use something, even if they no longer want to, simply because otherwise it will feel like a waste of money.

Why this Principle works:

To give an example, let's say a health club offers customers the option of paying for an annual membership. Whilst this one-off payment will help to reduce the pain of paying, as it condenses what could have been multiple payments into one simple transaction for a whole year, it also reduces the likelihood that they will continue to workout regularly and, ultimately, renew their membership next year. In studies, it's been shown that people who have annual memberships use them heavily for the first few months - whilst the amount they've paid is fresh in their minds - but when the Sunk-Cost Effect has dissipated, they use them infrequently (if at all). When this is the case, they are unlikely to renew. By contrast, people who pay for a monthly membership are repeatedly reminded of how much it is costing them. Therefore, the Sunk-Cost Effect stays intact and they are motivated to make the most of it. This level of interaction ultimately means they'll see the most benefits and be much more likely to extend their membership further.

How to use this Principle:

Paying for a subscription with a single payment lessens the Pain of Paying (Principle 41). However, sending regular emails to remind them what their annual membership is costing them per month could be key to encouraging consumption and thus retention, even if it does feel counter-intuitive.

Concrete Application Example:

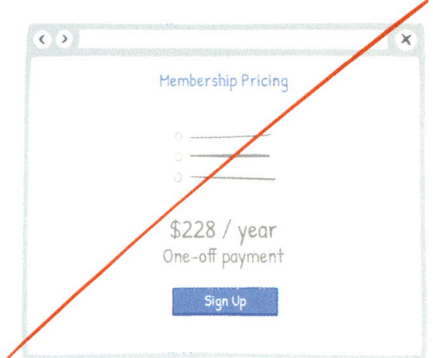
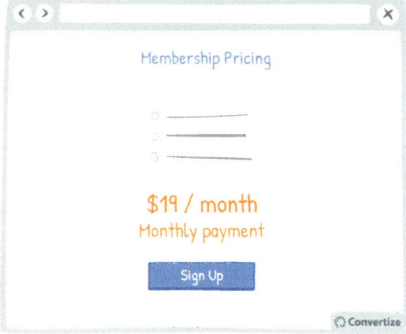

Rather than presenting a subscription as a yearly investment, which might seem frighteningly big at first and then disappear from your customers' minds, it can be more effective to present a subscription as a monthly cost. This will reduce the initial Pain of Paying and encourage customers to conceptualise the subscription in terms of repeated use. This could have a positive impact on customers' usage of your product or service and make them more likely to renew their subscription in the future.

Sources and further examples:

Sources:
- Gourville, 2002

Further examples on this PRIVATE page:
www.smart-persuasion.com/psychology-of-consumption

Reference Pricing

Principle 8

(Tversky & Kahneman, 1974; Green et al. 1998; Ariely, Loewenstein & Prelec, 2003; Nunes & Boatwright, 2004)

Description of the Principle:

It is human nature to compare and judge value based on comparisons, and the world of consumerism is no exception. Most people will only feel justified in purchasing something if its price matches the perceived value. This value can be changed according to how it is framed - as with Perceived Value Pricing (Principle 59) - and the use of Reference Pricing is one way in which framing a price can change our perception of value. Reference Pricing refers to the fact that individuals will decide what is a justifiable price to pay for a product or service by comparing it to other reference prices (such as competitors' pricing or previous, pre-sale pricing).

Why this Principle works:

For example, if you are told that an obscure vinyl record is on sale for $300, you won't really have any idea whether this is good value or not, as there is no point of market reference. If you then find out that another copy of the same record recently sold for almost $1000, you will have a new frame of reference.

How to use this Principle:

Research has shown that Reference Pricing comes into play on a subconscious level and that even the prices of unrelated products in close proximity can affect the perceived value of something. In a study conducted by Nunes & Boatwright (2004), CDs were placed on a beachside stall next to sweatshirts that were being sold alternately for $10 and $80 (at half hour intervals). When the sweatshirts were sold for $10 (Scenario A) people were only willing to pay $7.29 for the adjacent CDs, but when they were being sold at $80 (Scenario B), this price jumped almost 18% to $9! Without them even realising, customers were being influenced by the Reference Pricing of the completely unrelated sweatshirts.

In sales and marketing, Reference Pricing is a useful tool to help give products and services the desired value perception. By contrasting your prices with those of competitors or by highlighting how large a discount you are offering on a previously advertised price, customers will be likely to consider the purchase justified and, even more so, a good deal.

Concrete Application Example:

When offering discounted prices, it is essential to always still display the previous higher prices as well (crossed out is advisable to avoid confusion). Studies have shown that people tend to use the first piece of information they receive as an anchoring point to then judge subsequent information. In this way, showing the previous higher prices will ensure that their initial reference point is higher and will therefore help to make the current offered price seem even lower and cheaper than it actually is.

Leaving the previous prices displayed in this way will also highlight the deal that the customer is getting, increasing the chances that they will see it as a real bargain, not to be missed out on.

Sources and further examples:

Sources:
- Tversky & Kahneman, 1974; Green et al. 1998
- Ariely, Loewenstein & Prelec, 2003; Nunes & Boatwright, 2004

Further examples on this PRIVATE page:
www.smart-persuasion.com/reference-pricing

Zeigarnik Effect

(Zeigarnik, 1927)

Description of the Principle:

The Zeigarnik Effect is based on the idea that it is human nature to finish what we start and, if we don't manage to complete something, we experience an uncomfortable feeling of dissonance. This failure to finish something puts us in a state of tension that makes us pay more attention to the thing we want to finish. The consequence is that we remember uncompleted tasks more than completed tasks, and are often driven by this effect to complete something. In other words, we have little motivation to recall things we've finished, whereas we have a strong vested interest in unfinished things that keeps them at the forefront of our minds.

GREAT!
Only one more step left to finish.

Why this Principle works:

Russian psychologist Bluma Zeigarnik (after whom this effect is named) made note of this cognitive bias in a restaurant: she observed that waiters could remember complex food orders but, once a table had received their food and paid their bill, all the details would be forgotten. Waiters could easily call to mind the orders of those tables that were still "incomplete" (even if it had been some time since they'd taken their order or dealt with the table) whereas those of the "completed" tables were no longer in their memories. Once a table was taken care of, the details relating to it would disappear from the waiter's memory (in order to make way for new, or more relevant, information).

How to use this Principle:

The Zeigarnik Effect has many applications in the commercial world. For example, it is often employed by TV shows that use the "cliffhanger effect" to keep viewers engaged. It can also be used online to ensure customers complete a desired action. People will often complete a task that would otherwise cause them to feel the dissonance associated with this effect. Providing a clear and positive sense of progression and ultimate closure by displaying things such as progress bars can help to make your customers aware of how far along they are in a payment or sign-up process. This can encourage them to complete the process.

Concrete Application Example:

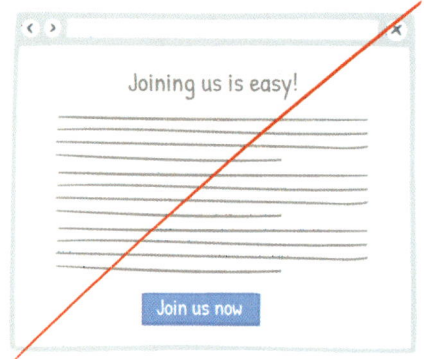 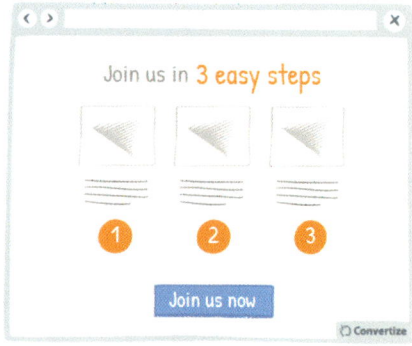

When you want a customer to complete a task that has multiple stages, such as signing up for an offer that requires more than one piece of information, or inputting payment and delivery details, set out these steps clearly.

As in the example above, visitors to your website will then understand exactly what they have to do to complete something and be more willing to invest time in achieving this.

It is also a good idea to include a progress bar with clearly marked stages that are shown to have been 'achieved' as a user progresses. This will remind them of previously completed tasks, thereby mitigating any tension associated with the tasks that remain.

Sources and further examples:

Sources:
- Zeigarnik, 1927

Further examples on this PRIVATE page:

www.smart-persuasion.com/zeigarnik-effect

Single-Option Aversion

(Mochon, 2013)

Description of the Principle:

Single-Option Aversion describes the way in which consumers are reluctant to pick an option - even one that they like - when no others are being offered. If you are presented with only one option, you will consider choosing this option to be potentially ill-informed or hasty. In other words, you are likely to think it better to consider alternative options before deciding to purchase, even if the single option available provides what you are looking for. This effect can lead to a product being chosen more often when competing alternatives are included than when it is offered alone.

Why this Principle works:

For example, if you walk into a store to buy a TV and there is only one model left, you are likely to prefer to look at other options before making the purchase, even if the TV available seems to be a good product. This is especially true of more expensive items. Daniel Mochon demonstrated the Single-Option Aversion with an experiment in which he offered the hypothetical purchase of a DVD player to participants. His study showed that just 9% of participants said they would buy the Sony model offered when it was the only option whereas the percentage went up to 32% when the same model was offered alongside a Philips model.

How to use this Principle:

This principle is an important consideration when deciding how many options you should present to your customers. It is better not to offer an overly limited choice to your customers, as this is likely to motivate them to look for alternatives. This could lead to them making the purchase in another store. However, you don't want to overwhelm them with options either, as this can lead to indecision due to the Paradox of Choice (Principle 30). So it is important to consider carefully how you group your products.

Concrete Application Example:

 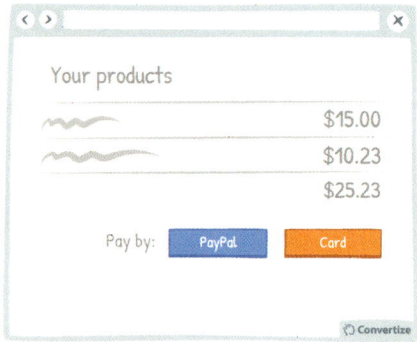

This example shows that Single-Option Aversion also applies to the later stages of the sales funnel. Your customers will appreciate having several payment options. Giving them the choice between paying through PayPal or with a credit card is an easy way to increase the options available to them.

Whilst it may seem like a distraction from the ultimate conversion to include alternative payment options, the additional choice will prevent some hesitant visitors from delaying their purchase. Furthermore, the options your customers choose will provide you with information about what type of payment solution they prefer. You can then advertise them more prominently throughout your site.

Sources and further examples:

Sources:
- Mochon, 2013

Further examples on this PRIVATE page:
www.smart-persuasion.com/single-option-aversion

Principle 11

Mere-Exposure Effect

(Fechner, 1876; Zajonc, 1968)

Description of the Principle:

First explored by Gustav Fechner in the 19th Century, our understanding of the Mere-Exposure Effect was further developed between 1960-1990 by renowned psychologist Robert Zajonc. He discovered that people react more favourably to certain things the more they are exposed to them.

Why this Principle works:

Humans are naturally more comfortable with, and positive towards, things that they are familiar with. People are more likely to react positively to something familiar than something unexpected. Responses to a brand or product can often be improved simply through repeated exposure. One of Zajonc's experiments consisted of showing people nonsense characters that looked like Chinese symbols and asking them to guess the meaning. After they had been shown the same symbols several times, the meanings offered become more and more positive as, even subconsciously, people had become more familiar with those symbols.

How to use this Principle:

In marketing, the Mere-Exposure Effect can be used in many ways. Of course, you want to stand out to a certain extent, but being too different from the brands that people are already familiar with could result in distrust. You can make your own brand seem more familiar, and therefore more trustworthy, by basing it on those which already have a loyal following.

Another way to use the Mere-Exposure Effect is to employ a famous person to help promote your brand. Celebrity endorsements are successful not because that celebrity is an expert on the product or industry, but because they have a familiar face. We are immediately drawn towards them and the product they are representing.

Concrete Application Example:

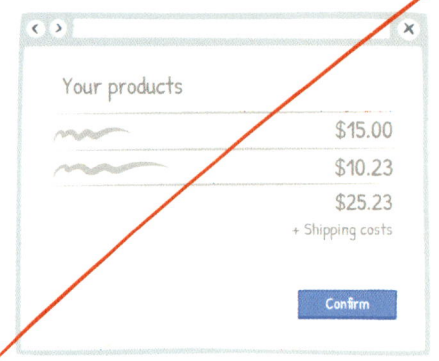 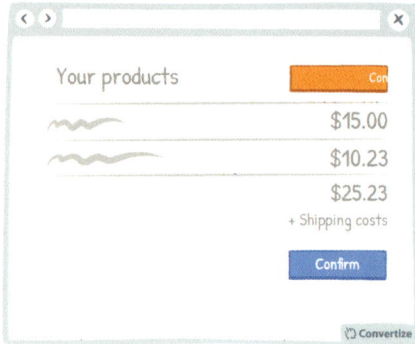

It is almost always better to display your Call To Action (CTA) as a button rather than a simple link as it will both attract your user's attention and make it clear that it is a CTA ready to be clicked on.

It is also a good idea to display your primary CTA more than once on a page. Of course, displaying it twice, or even multiple times, will increase the likelihood of people noticing it and reduce the risk of the CTA simply being missed.

By offering the CTA to people at different moments (for example, at the top and bottom of the page) you increase the chance that it is available at the time a visitor feels most inclined to act; perhaps they weren't ready to go through to the next step when they first arrived on the page, but are after reading its contents. By placing a duplicate CTA at the bottom of the screen, you make it easy for them to click immediately (rather than needing to scroll back up and look for the button again).

Studies also show that people react more positively towards stimuli that they have been exposed to several times. The stimulus becomes familiar, and we are more likely to engage with the familiar. So showing the CTA button two or more times will allow for this bias to occur and increase your chances that users end up clicking.

Sources and further examples:

Sources:
- Fechner, 1876
- Zajonc, 1968
- Schwartz, 2004

Further examples on this PRIVATE page:
www.smart-persuasion.com/mere-exposure-effect

Principle 12

Serial Position Effect

(Ebbinghaus, 1913; Murdock, 1962; Glanzer & Cunitz, 1966)

Description of the Principle:

The Serial Position Effect (notably studied by Ebbinghaus, Murdock, Glanzer and Cunitz) refers to the finding that recall accuracy will vary as a result of where an item is positioned within a list. Items are more likely to be remembered if they are presented at the beginning (the primacy effect) or the end (the recency effect) of a list, relative to those items presented in the middle. We more easily remember the first few items because of the greater amount of cerebral processing devoted to them, and we remember the last few items more easily because they are still in our short-term memory when recall is needed. Items that benefit from neither of these effects (the middle items) are recalled most poorly.

Why this Principle works:

To give an example, the Serial Position Effect can be observed when you go the supermarket after having only been given a verbal list of items to buy. In the time it takes to get there (and with all the distractions available as you wander the aisles) you will probably forget some of the items on the list. You will tend to remember the first few, as your brain was actively processing these as they were told to you, and the ones you heard more recently before you left.

How to use this Principle:

The Serial Position Effect has many applications within advertising and marketing. Taking this principle into account is important for TV advertising as it helps to determine which commercial break, and which position within each break, will be most valuable for an advertiser. It is also important for online advertising, as it suggests where on a webpage an advert is likely to receive maximum attention. A famous study completed in 2006 showed that links at the top and bottom of a website menu receive the most clicks. When structuring marketing content it is best to place the most important links at the top and bottom.

Concrete Application Example:

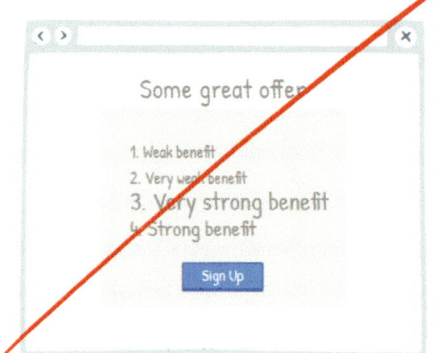 

Re-ordering the benefits of your offer, by putting the strongest ones first, will make it much more likely to capture people's attention. Research has shown that people recall the first items in a series best.

If listed first, your visitors will remember the stronger benefits because of the greater amount of cognitive attention and processing devoted to them.

Sources and further examples:

Sources:
- Ebbinghaus, 1913
- Murdock, 1962
- Glanzer & Cunitz, 1966

Further examples on this PRIVATE page:

www.smart-persuasion.com/serial-position-effect

Focusing Effect

(Schkade & Kahneman, 1998)

Description of the Principle:

The Focusing Effect is the way in which the human mind places too much emphasis on certain limited factors when making decisions. Instead of taking into account the less distinctive (but perhaps more important) factors when making a choice, we only recognise and place value on a few obvious pieces of information. This causes an imbalance in judgment, and often leads to misinformed evaluations.

Why this Principle works:

In a study carried out by Schkade & Kahneman (1998) where people were asked whether Californians or Mid-Westerners led happier lives, participants overwhelmingly assumed and stated that it was Californians. They were, of course, falling victim to the Focusing Effect and basing their decision on familiar clichés about better weather and more relaxed lifestyles. However, in reality, this is not the case as there is no discernible difference between the happiness of residents in these two areas.

By putting emphasis on a limited number of factors, other more important determinants of happiness were overlooked, such as crime rates and safety from natural disasters.

How to use this Principle:

In the commercial arena, the Focusing Effect is often utilised as a selling technique. Knowing that people are more likely to understand the value of something if it is based on a few simple factors, has a significant effect on the way marketers promote their products. Consumers are looking for products that will improve their lives in an obvious way and are most receptive to clear, concise and specific value propositions. Focusing on only a few key components of the product you are trying to sell, specifically on the most widely recognisable or most distinctive features, is good way of leveraging the Focusing Effect in your marketing.

Concrete Application Example:

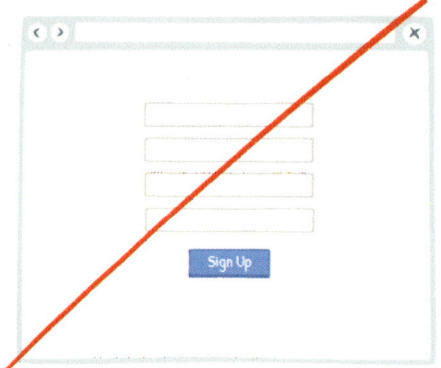 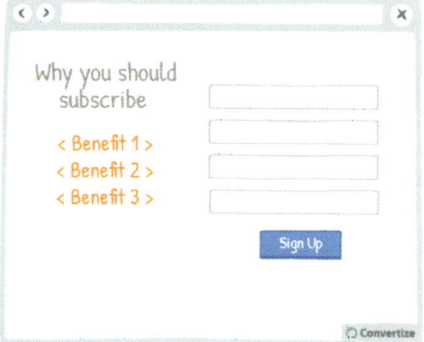

If you do not offer a guest checkout option, you should clearly explain to your customers the advantages of registering (to encourage them to take the time to do so).

By showcasing just the 3 main benefits, you can make your point clear, unambiguous and simple to digest, which will give you more chance of convincing your customers that it is worth their while to register.

For example, if your SaaS product is best-known for effectively defending against malware, make sure to emphasise this. Your customers will be more persuaded by a consistent message, repeated throughout your marketing materials, than by a long list of claims.

People are likely to make decisions just based on one or two distinguishable features, and so if you can reinforce one of the benefits at this stage, they may make their decision to act based on this one thing alone.

Sources and further examples:

Sources:
- Schkade & Kahneman, 1998

Further examples on this PRIVATE page:

www.smart-persuasion.com/focusing-effect

Principle 14

Partitioned Pricing

(Morwitz, Greenleaf, & Johnson, 1998; Hossain & Morgan, 2006)

Description of the Principle:

In their research paper "Divide and Prosper: Consumers' Reactions to Partitioned Prices", Morwitz, Greenleaf, & Johnson (1998) explore the effect that splitting the total price of a purchase into two (or even potentially more) parts can have on consumer behaviour: this is called Partitioned Pricing.

In most cases, your typical consumer is unlikely to undertake the cognitive effort required to accurately add the separate components together before they make the decision to purchase. The "base price" – being the cost of the product itself – is often the only part customers notice. Any "surcharges" – additional costs that are presented separately, such as shipping, handling or taxes – are mentally discarded. If your customers do calculate the full amount, they will often use rounded-down numbers that make for more manageable sums.

However, the opposite effect can occur if all components of the partitioned pricing aren't made salient. This can make the customer feel as though they are being misled, which will lead to no purchase at all, or an unhappy post-sale situation. For example, let's say you are offered a cruise for $100, and this is the only visible cost throughout the initial stages of the purchasing process.

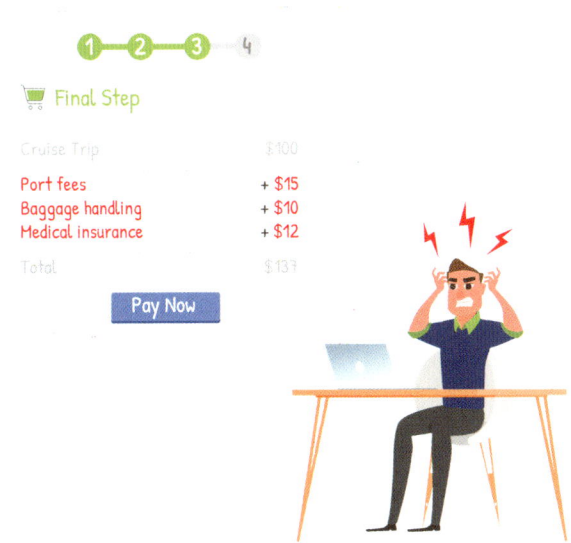

Then, port fees, baggage handling, and medical insurance are suddenly made apparent at the final payment page. This unexpected escalation in cost is likely to disrupt the purchase, as well as leading to possible anger at the misrepresentation.

This is why it is important to ensure that the majority of costs are included in the "base price", so that any additional surcharges are too trivial to affect the decision to purchase.

How to use this Principle:

In online marketing, this can be a useful tool to help increase conversion rates. Reducing the perceived pricing of a product by not including delivery charges or obligatory handling fees in the main product price listing will, of course, make the pricing seem more competitive and attractive. The customer will then base their decision to purchase on the product price alone. Having additional costs presented separately can make it seem like a better deal, despite the overall amount being the same.

Concrete Application Example:

 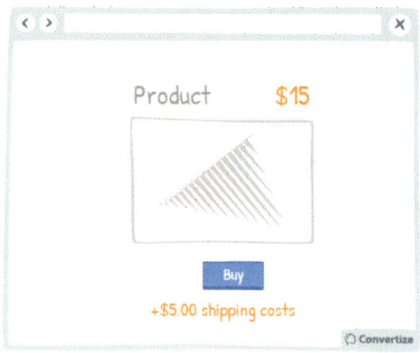

Separating the product price from other smaller charges - such as delivery costs or handling fees - will help to give the impression of a lower overall price. The first price seen will stick in the customer's mind. If they have already decided that they want to buy the product, before seeing the minor surcharges, they are unlikely to expend extra mental effort in reassessing its value.

If you are offering a special discount on delivery, or even a free delivery (which appears as a charge with a line crossing it out), then separating charges out in this way is still a good idea. It allows you to really highlight the offer, and might give people who are still unsure a nudge to complete their purchase.

Sources and further examples:

Sources:
- Taylor & Fiske, 1978
- Morwitz, Greenleaf, & Johnson, 1998
- Hossain & Morgan, 2006

Further examples on this PRIVATE page:
www.smart-persuasion.com/partitioned-pricing

Principle 15

Default Effect

(Johnson, Hershey, Meszaros & Kunreuther, 1993)

Description of the Principle:

The Default Effect was most notably studied by Johnson, Hershey, Meszaros & Kunreuther (1993) and demonstrates how having a "default choice" available influences our decisions. Amongst all the options given to us when we need to make a choice, the default choice is the one that doesn't require us to actually make any active decision: it has already been chosen for us. For example, when we install software on our computer, we're usually offered a default installation option. When selected, we only need to continue with the installation in a passive manner, with all the functions chosen for us. This is by far the most popular (non-) choice made. The Default Effect is the way in which any default option on offer is more likely to be chosen over anything else, and so offering up a default option gives us a powerful way of influencing people's decisions.

Why this Principle works:

Scientists believe this comes down to multiple reasons. Firstly, opting for a passive choice requires the least mental effort, whereas comparing and weighing up different options can mean a lot of time spent evaluating. When we are having a hard time deliberating between several similar options, choosing the default option requires the least mental effort. This allows us to minimise the large number of choices we face every day and therefore focus on more important decisions.

We are also more likely to choose default options as we assume that they have been recommended. In the case of the computer software installation, decisions about technical preferences might seem too specialised or complicated for us. We expect that the default option has been set up by someone with more expertise than us, and that it is most likely to be appropriate to our requirements.

Looking at default choices can also reveal how often we are likely to accept a default choice without question, whereas, if asked to actively consider the decision and make a more thoughtful choice, we might not agree. For example, scientific studies carried out regarding the relation of the Default Effect on organ donation found that there are less donors in countries where consent is not given by default. If you are simply put on the organ donor list by default because you haven't actively expressed that you do not wish to be one, you probably would never even really consider this.

By contrast, if you were asked to actively give your consent, you would be more prone to start thinking about it in detail and might become more emotionally involved and less likely to agree.

In web marketing, the Default Effect can come into play whenever your customer needs to make a decision, whether that be about signing up to your newsletter, or choosing a product or method of delivery. Offering a default option when there is a choice you would rather they make (e.g. making sure that boxes to opt people in to receive your offers are always pre-ticked) will increase the likelihood of visitors making that choice.

Concrete Application Example:

If you have a particular option or add-on that you would like your customers to choose, making it a default option will greatly increase the chances of them doing so. Default options are so attractive because they offer a passive choice, which is often preferable to the cognitive effort of making our own decisions. We also tend to view a default option as "the most popular", choosing to believe that it is pre-selected because it is in-demand and therefore more valuable. We like to choose the same things as others as it makes us feel safe in our choices.

Finally, highlighting a default option will automatically draw attention to the benefits and features offered there. After seeing this, the act of changing to a cheaper, smaller package will trigger loss aversion, causing people to feel as though they are missing out on those things that the default option offers.

Sources and further examples:

Sources:
- Johnson, Hershey, Meszaros & Kunreuther, 1993

Further examples on this PRIVATE page:
www.smart-persuasion.com/default-effect

Principle 16

Magnitude Encoding Process

(Oppenheimer, LeBoeuf & Brewer, 2007;
Coulter & Coulter, 2005; Thomas & Morwitz, 2005)

Description of the Principle:

If you want people to perceive a price as being small, then it can be very effective to associate all of its features with a small magnitude, including the way it is visually presented. Numerical stimuli (prices included) are represented and encoded in our memories as magnitude representations (i.e., judgments of relative "size"). Therefore, if you want a number or price to be perceived as smaller, it is possible to influence this through the way it is physically represented.

Why this Principle works:

Research has shown that judgments are often made based on irrelevant anchors (Principle 3) but Oppenheimer, LeBoeuf and Brewer (2007) found that this also extends to physical and visual anchors. In other words, people will be biased in making judgments depending on any associated visual stimulus. In their experiment, the unrelated small visual stimulus presented resulted in people having smaller numerical values in mind. They conducted an experiment whereby students were given three drawn lines (1 straight, 1 wavy and 1 an inverted "u" shape) and asked to copy these without use of a ruler.

Group A were given short lines and Group B longer lines. The second section of the experiment consisted of a questionnaire, where the first question was: "How many miles long is the Mississippi River?" This was followed by 5 random questions (to avoid anyone catching on to the reasoning behind the test).

The results showed that Group A, who had drawn shorter lines, gave an average response of 72 miles. Group B, who had drawn longer lines, gave an average response of 1224 miles. This huge difference was entirely due to the length of the lines they were first asked to draw.

The researchers later repeated the experiment, changing the question to: "What is the average temperature in Fahrenheit in Honolulu, Hawaii?" Once again, Group A (with the shorter lines) gave a much lower number than Group B. This shows that the physical anchor used in magnitude encoding doesn't have to be visually similar to the quantity subjects are estimating.

Concrete Application Example:

Using a smaller font size for your pricing is doubly effective. Firstly, it of course makes the price more subtle and so doesn't automatically draw people's attention towards the fact of paying and how much money they will have to part with to have the product.

Secondly, it has been proven that we associate small visual stimuli with small numerical values. The smaller the physical size of the price, the smaller people will perceive the price to be.

Sources and further examples:

Sources:
- Worchel, Lee & Adewole, 1975
- Thomas & Morwitz, 2005
- Coulter & Coulter, 2005
- Oppenheimer, LeBouf & Brewer, 2007

Further examples on this PRIVATE page:
www.smart-persuasion.com/magnitude-encoding-process

Principle 17

Time vs Money Effect

(Mogilner & Aaker, 2009)

Description of the Principle:

The Time vs Money Effect was notably studied by Mogilner and Aaker in 2009. They showed that people react much more favourably to sales pitches that make reference to time rather than money. We react much more positively to references to the time we will get to spend with a product than any mention of money (even if that is to say how much money we might save).

Why this Principle works:

Mogilner and Aaker put forward several reasons to explain the Time vs Money Effect. Firstly, we have a much more personal relationship with time than with money. Describing the time we might spend enjoying a product creates a more immediate emotional and personal connection with it.

Time is also a rare resource, and isn't replaceable like money. Once time is spent, we can't get it back - which increases its value. Therefore, if we think that using this product is a worthwhile way of passing our time, it will immediately go up in our estimations. Finally, by concentrating on our future use of a product and not on the price, we are less likely to dwell for too long on its monetary value. More specifically, we are unlikely to wonder if it is in fact too expensive or overpriced. The Pain of Paying (Principle 41) has shown that the act of spending money significantly decreases our pleasure in purchasing. Therefore, it is always more effective to concentrate on another aspect of the purchase when marketing your products.

How to use this Principle:

Mogilner and Aaker conducted many experiments to test this principle. In one of them, they split students from Stanford University who owned iPods into 3 groups. The first group was asked: "How much money have you spent on your iPod?" The second group was asked: "How much time have you spent on your iPod?" The third group was not asked a preliminary question. Each of the groups were then asked to complete a questionnaire. The second group, who had been reminded about the amount of time they spent using their iPod, gave by far the most favourable opinions and feedback about the product.

The Time vs Money Effect is important to bear in mind when marketing your products. It may be more effective to discuss the benefits a user will receive when using it, rather than concentrating on any financial offers or other price-based selling points. However, you should bear in mind that for some products, discounts are more effective than descriptions of how much the consumer will enjoy it. This is often true of cheaper essential goods.

Concrete Application Example:

 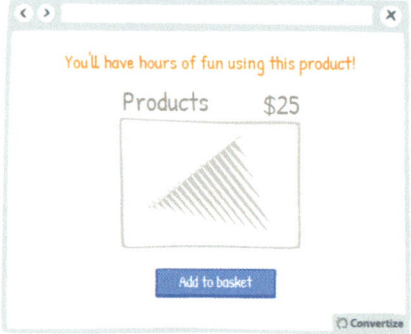

It is best to avoid references to money when presenting your products to customers. Instead, emphasise the benefits they will experience by using them. People place more value on experiences than on money, and focusing on this will allow them to connect with your product or service. The subsequent connection with the product will be more emotional and effective. This also allows you to avoid any reference to the money they have to spend to get it (even if you are pointing out a saving, it still draws attention to the fact of having to pay).

Sources and further examples:

Sources:
- Baron, Beattie & Hershey, 1988
- Mogilner & Aaker, 2009

Further examples on this PRIVATE page:
www.smart-persuasion.com/time-versus-money-effect

Recency Effect

Principle 18

(Ebbinghaus, 1913; Miller & Campbell, 1959; Murdock, 1962; Glanzer & Cunitz, 1966)

Description of the Principle:

The Recency Effect is a cognitive bias that explains why it is easiest to remember the last piece of information we received. Of course, the information that we read or heard most recently will be clearest in our short-term memories and will be recalled most easily. For example, if someone asks you to complete a long list of tasks, you are more likely to remember the last thing on the list than those that came at the beginning or in the middle.

Why this Principle works:

We give immediate significance to the most recent pieces of information, subconsciously preferring them over anything that came before. This phenomenon explains our relationship with "novelty" items. The Novelty Effect describes the way in which new products have a short-term advantage over more established products. We prefer them simply because they are new and different. Looking at this in terms of a website, if a new function/page/tab is created, visitors are more likely to click on it or interact with it as desired, and also to view it in a favourable light.

How to use this Principle:

Many companies play to this bias by updating their products regularly. In doing so, they benefit from both the Recency Effect and the Novelty Effect. One example is the way that Apple releases new iPhones on a regular basis, being fully aware that, even if the new model doesn't include many different features, it will generate excitement simply because it is novel.

Concrete Application Example:

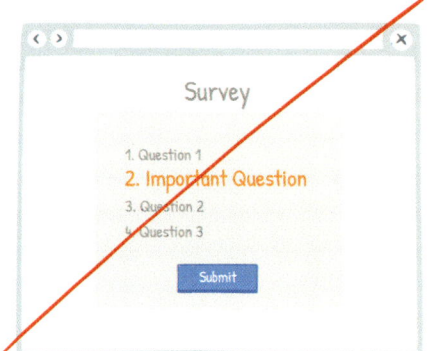
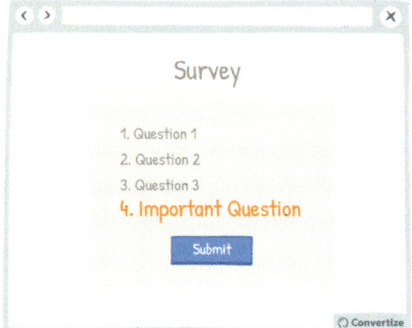

Re-ordering a list of items or questions and placing the most important ones last will make them more memorable.

Research has shown that people recall the last items in a series best, and sometimes don't even really take in information presented prior. If listed first or last, your visitors will remember the questions better because of the greater amount of cogntive attention and processing devoted to them.

Sources and further examples:

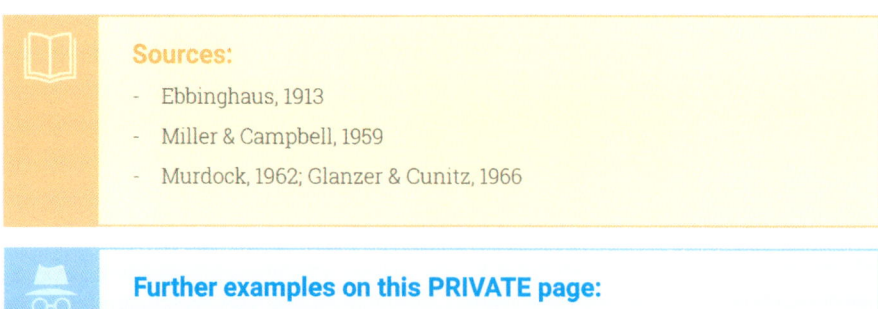

Sources:
- Ebbinghaus, 1913
- Miller & Campbell, 1959
- Murdock, 1962; Glanzer & Cunitz, 1966

Further examples on this PRIVATE page:
www.smart-persuasion.com/recency-effect

Principle 19

Cheerleader Effect

(Walker & Vul, 2013)

Description of the Principle:

The Cheerleader Effect is the way in which, when confronted with a group of items, the human brain automatically treats them as a set and forms an impression of this set as a whole. We generate average information on everything we are viewing - including the setting, size, emotions conveyed (in animate objects) and attractiveness - and then make a visual judgment based on these averages. Therefore, those items that may be less attractive or desirable find that they are elevated in status to the average that has already been accepted.

Why this Principle works:

This is called the Cheerleader Effect as it is a phenomenon notably perceived in the way that people are considered more attractive when they are in a group than when they are seen alone. Walker and Vul conducted a series of studies on the effect in 2013. Participants were presented with a selection of photographs showing various strangers' faces. Each face was seen twice: once alone and once in a group. In every case, their attractiveness was rated higher when displayed in the group photos. The effect is due to the way our visual system makes sense of seeing multiple items: by choosing the most positive features from all and combining them to make one easy-to-digest ensemble.

How to use this Principle:

The Cheerleader Effect is particularly significant for marketers, as it can affect the way a product is perceived. Not only does the effect take place automatically, but it is very hard for us to override - even when we are aware of it.

The effect is used for optimizing product pages. It is often more effective to show pictures of a product as part of a collection than to display it on its own. Seen as part of a group, the appeal of the item is increased as the viewer combines its positive qualities with those of the surrounding objects.

Concrete Application Example:

 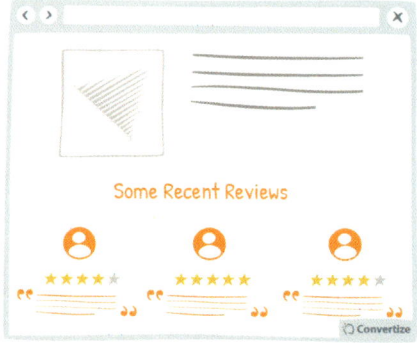

It is important to show potential customers that your products are well-reviewed. However, hiding negative reviews is a bad strategy. Customers will realise that the information you have displayed is not representative, and will begin to distrust your website.

Using the Cheerleader Effect can help you to mediate the impact of negative feedback. If you present testimonials in a group setting, the best reviews will compensate for the less positive ones. That way, any negative comments or low ratings will not deter your visitors. Instead, visitors will appreciate your transparency and put greater trust in your website.

Sources and further examples:

Sources:
- Walker & Vul, 2013

Further examples on this PRIVATE page:
www.smart-persuasion.com/cheerleader-effect

Needs and Motivation

How to address intrinsic and extrinsic needs and motivate your visitors to act

Principle 20

Self-Efficacy Theory

(Bandura, 1984)

Description of the Principle:

Self-Efficacy, first defined by Albert Bandura (1984), shows that our perception of our own ability to complete a task affects our subsequent behaviour and our ability to succeed. In other words, the more competent we think we are, the greater our intrinsic motivation is to act. High or low self-efficacy determines whether or not someone will choose to take on a challenging task or perceive it as impossible to complete.

According to Bandura's theory, people with a high level of self-efficacy are more likely to view difficult tasks as something to be mastered, rather than something to be avoided. Different factors can influence our self-efficacy; such as past successful experiences for similar tasks, positive feedback, or "vicarious experiences" (when we see others being successful in a task).

Why this Principle works:

A scientific study revealed this effect by studying two groups of students engaged in solving puzzles over 3 different sessions. Group A received positive feedback after their first session, whereas Group B did not. The results then overwhelmingly showed that Group A went on to be more motivated and successful in the subsequent tasks than Group B.

How to use this Principle:

Self-Efficacy Theory can be used in online marketing in order to increase visitors' motivation and self-confidence when they are asked to complete a task online. For example, creating "vicarious experiences" by displaying details of customers who have previously taken a desired action (such as buying something or writing a review) is a good way to encourage others to do the same. It will also increase their belief in their own ability to complete the action.

Concrete Application Example:

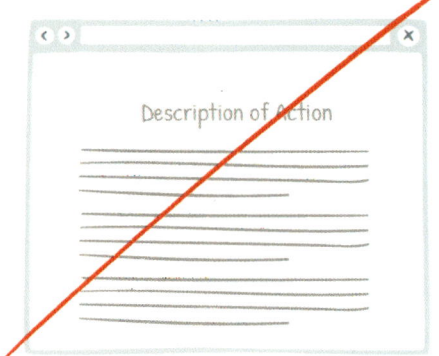 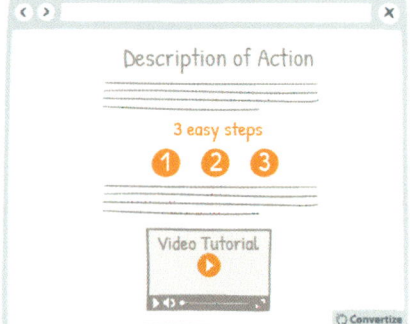

If you show your visitors how easy it is for them to act (i.e. to complete an action on your website or to utilise one of your products or services) by providing "how-to" pages and videos, it will increase their belief in their own competence to do so.

This will consequently increase their motivation to do it as research has shown that the more confident we feel in our own abilities, the greater our intrinsic motivation to act.

Sources and further examples:

Sources:
- Bandura, 1984

Further examples on this PRIVATE page:
www.smart-persuasion.com/self-efficacy-theory

Principle 21

Need for Certainty

(Kagan, 1972)

Description of the Principle:

In 1976, the developmental psychologist Jerome Kagan outlined six basic human needs. One of them, which every human experiences, is the Need for Certainty. The Need for Certainty comes from the fact that our brain likes to know what is going on and feel in control of its interactions by recognising patterns. Indeed, feeling more certain about the world around us leads to positive feelings of control and security. Moreover, when the craving for certainty is met, there is a sensation of reward. The ability to predict something and then obtain data that confirms those predictions results in a positive feeling. That's why some people experience a feeling of accomplishment after cleaning their house or organising things: it provides a reassuring sense of certainty. By contrast, the brain reacts negatively towards uncertainty, leading us to feel alert, anxious and uncomfortable.

Why this Principle works:

Paradoxically, the tension we feel when we are uncertain can also have a positive effect. Uncertainty can inspire creativity and provide the spontaneity and variety that we crave as humans. Because of this, both certainty and uncertainty are human needs that have to exist in balance.

How to use this Principle:

This theory has many important applications in marketing. Providing your customers with certainty in the form of reassuring information is a simple way to earn their trust. Entire industries exist to provide paying customers with an increased level of certainty (for example, through expert advice or predictions). When designing a website, you should eliminate any uncertainty that your users might experience. Provide clear instructions, tell them what is going to happen at every stage, list the information and the credentials they will (and won't) need, be specific and consistent when reinforcing the credibility of your offer (either through user numbers or testimonials). Don't expect them to draw conclusions for themselves and don't make them think.

Concrete Application Example:

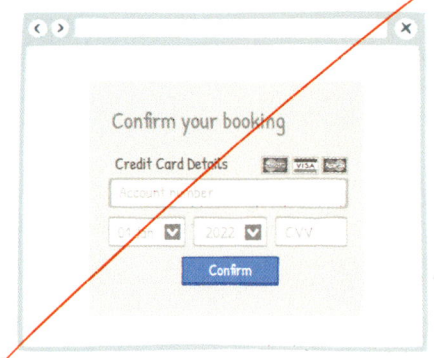 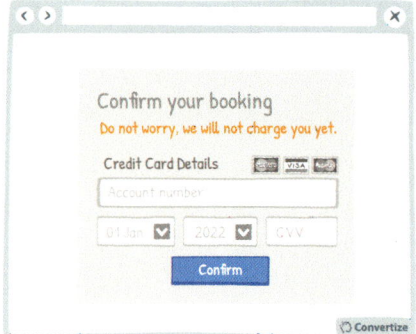

The Need for Certainty is particularly significant during moments of stress. A customer who is making a difficult choice or navigating a payment page will feel reassured by information that removes any doubt or ambiguity.

Making the payment process transparent, by letting customers know how and when they will be charged, is a simple way to reduce uncertainty. By doing so, your customers will be more likely to complete a purchase and less likely to abandon their shopping cart.

Sources and further examples:

Sources:
- Kagan, 1972

Further examples on this PRIVATE page:
www.smart-persuasion.com/need-for-certainty-uncertainty

Ben Franklin Effect

(Jecker & Landy, 1969; Limperos et al., 2014)

Description of the Principle:

The Ben Franklin Effect is named after the well-known figure of American history, Benjamin Franklin. He is quoted as having said the following: "He that has once done you a kindness will be more ready to do you another than he whom you yourself have obliged." The Ben Franklin Effect, demonstrated by numerous psychological studies, describes the way in which doing someone a favour leads us to feel more favourable towards them. The effect makes us more inclined to do them a second or third favour.

We can follow the reasoning that if we have agreed to do them a favour, it must be because we like them (even when that's not strictly the case) and so we subconsciously decide to like them even more in order to be consistent with our behaviour. Conversely, if we act in a negative way towards someone, then we justify it to ourselves as being because they aren't nice or worthy of good treatment.

Why this Principle works:

Contrary to our usual assumption that our feelings towards someone will dictate how we treat them, the Ben Franklin Effect shows that our behaviour towards someone can actually dictate how we feel about them. In fact, if you can encourage people to act kindly towards you, they will begin to feel more kindly towards you, too.

In his autobiography, Benjamin Franklin illustrated this point with an example from his own life. Remembered from the 1730s, when he started his political career, Franklin's story shows how an "enemy" can be won round by asking them for help. There was one Assemblyman who didn't care for Franklin at all. However, Franklin knew that his political career depended on the man's support. He asked the man if he could simply borrow one of the books from his private library. The request was calculated to flatter the man (especially as Franklin was renowned in the literary world for being a successful printer and writer). As expected, the man lent him the book and this small act of kindness led to the two becoming good friends.

How to use this Principle:

The Ben Franklin Effect is used regularly in sales strategies, the most well-known being the Foot-in-the-door Technique (Principle 31). This consists of asking someone for a small agreement in order to later get a more significant one. Studies conducted by Limperos et al. (2014) have shown ways in which the Ben Franklin Effect can be applied to social media, for example through friend requests on Facebook.

Concrete Application Example:

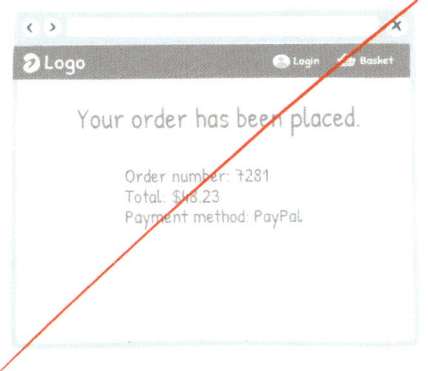 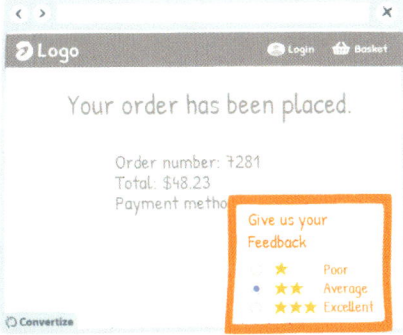

It has been proven that people enjoy giving their opinion and being asked for feedback. What's more, if you ask for this using a short, easy-to-complete survey, you increase your chances that people will do this for you. Succeeding in this is doubly useful: firstly, you will receive some helpful feedback that you can then implement to improve your site and services, and secondly, you will boost your own likability.

This is because, as studies have shown, people who carry out a favour or "service" for someone are much more likely to take away a positive impression of that person.

Therefore, getting your customers to complete a survey for your product will boost their positive feelings towards your brand and site, which will ultimately lead to them coming back to make further purchases with you.

Sources and further examples:

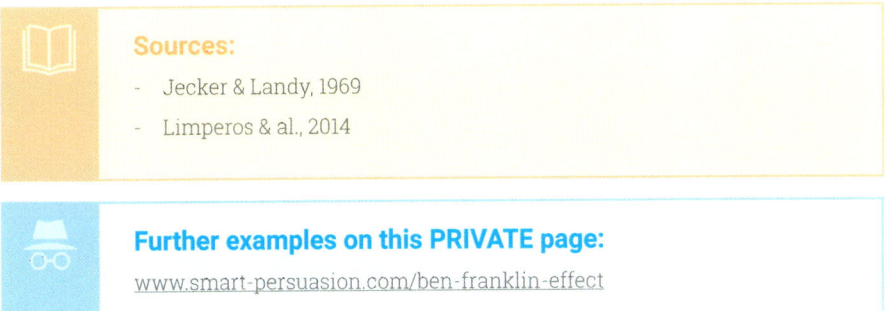

Principle 23

Cognitive Ease

(Kahneman, 2011)

Description of the Principle:

Cognitive Ease or fluency is the measure of how easy it is for our brains to process information. The cognitive ease of something will alter how we feel about it, and affects how motivated we are to invest our time and effort in it. The behavioural economist and Nobel Prize winner Daniel Kahneman explains in his book *Thinking, Fast and Slow* (2011) that our brains have two modes of thinking. System 1 operates automatically and quickly, with little or no effort and no sense of voluntary control. It is the mental function that occurs when you see a word and instantly interpret it. System 2 is engaged when we are required to pay more conscious attention to the information presented. To give an example, we have to allocate the specific mental effort of System 2 to solve complex mathematical calculations.

Why this Principle works:

When Cognitive Ease is reduced because the mental effort required is too much, we engage this second system of "effortful mental activity" and switch to a state of cognitive strain. The Cognitive Ease principle reveals that when people have to switch to the second system of thinking, the cognitive strain makes them more vigilant and suspicious. It results in a decrease in the confidence, trust, and pleasure involved in completing the mental action. In other words, people are happier and more receptive towards familiar and easily understandable situations in which they feel safer, more confident and at ease.

How to use this Principle:

To give an example, the way reduced prices are written during a sale will greatly affect people's attitude towards the products (and their likelihood of purchasing them). If the sale prices are easy to understand using percentages (for example, "- 50%") or with the new prices already calculated (for example, "now only $20"), shoppers will react in an automatic and positive fashion. However, if it is necessary for them to do complex mental calculations (for example, if a $27.50 product is advertised at 12% off), they will switch to a more analytical style of thinking.

This results in more attention spent on the calculation, and subsequently on the merits of the product. No longer feeling spontaneous, your customer will start questioning whether it is actually a good deal or not, whether they really need another pair of shoes, etc. The more cerebral effort we demand from our customers, the more of a negative and suspicious reaction we will evoke, and our chances of making a sale diminish.

The Cognitive Ease principle has many applications in marketing. For example, psychological studies have found that shares in companies with easier-to-pronounce names perform better than those with difficult-to-pronounce names. In online marketing, any possible elements that can simplify a website should be used: infographics, intuitive web design, easy-to-read font, and so on.

Concrete Application Example:

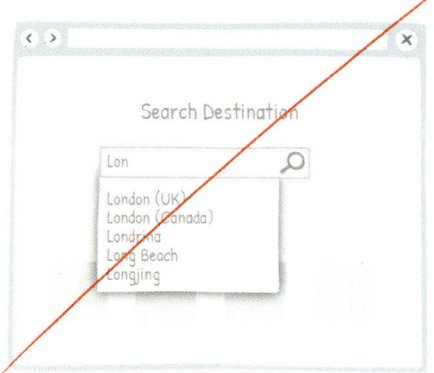 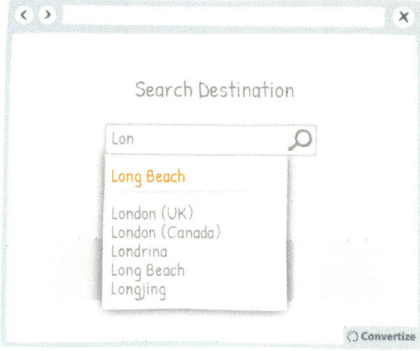

When a user begins a search, start by showing them previous searches they have made that correspond. Displaying these first and perhaps in a different colour to really distinguish them is a good way of helping a user to keep track of what they have previously done on your site. Personalising your website in this way will make it more intuitive and easier to use.

The easier-to-use and more adaptive your site is, the more likely people will be to enjoy using it and be encouraged to convert and come back again.

Sources and further examples:

Sources:
- Kahneman, 2011

Further examples on this PRIVATE page:
www.smart-persuasion.com/cognitive-ease

Principle 24

Curse of Knowledge

(Camerer, Loewenstein & Weber, 1989; Newton, 1990)

Description of the Principle:

The Curse of Knowledge was first studied by economists Camerer, Loewenstein & Weber in 1989. This cognitive bias leads people who are better informed on a subject to find it almost impossible to consider that subject from the point of view of someone who doesn't know as much about it. This often means that concepts, ideas and information aren't presented clearly enough, because the person presenting it presumes a certain level of knowledge and comprehension from their audience.

Why this Principle works:

Once you know something, it is impossible to put that knowledge aside. You also forget that not everyone has the same information as you. As a result, you will see and experience things differently, making it difficult to anticipate their needs. Psychologist Elizabeth Newton conducted a famous experiment demonstrating this effect in 1990. Participants were divided into two groups, with one group "tapping" well-known songs whilst the other group listened and attempted to identify them. The group who were tapping estimated a successful guess rate of at least 50% whilst the outcome was actually only 2.5%. The fact that those who were tapping the songs already knew which song it was – and, of course, could hear this song in their heads whilst tapping – meant that they were biased towards believing the answer was obvious. They couldn't understand why the other group found it so difficult to guess the song. Of course, the group listening was just hearing a series of discordant and therefore mostly unidentifiable taps.

How to use this Principle:

The implications of this in the commercial world are widespread as it is often a well-informed party who sets pricing for an object or service (a wine expert picks and values wine, a dressmaker sets prices for luxury fabrics etc.) Due to the Curse of Knowledge, companies find themselves unable to anticipate how lesser-informed customers will perceive their valuation. This often leads to high-quality goods being overpriced for the market and low-quality goods being underpriced.

It is also essential to be aware of - and to try and counteract - the bias of the Curse of Knowledge in any kind of business communications. Everyone who works for a certain company will have a comparatively advanced level of knowledge of what that company does. However, it is important to remember that the people you are communicating with outside of your company – customers, other businesses, or even other people within the same field – may not necessarily understand certain phrases, systems, or ideas. Keeping communications clear and easily comprehensible for everyone is an important factor in making your website and services both accessible and engaging.

Concrete Application Example:

 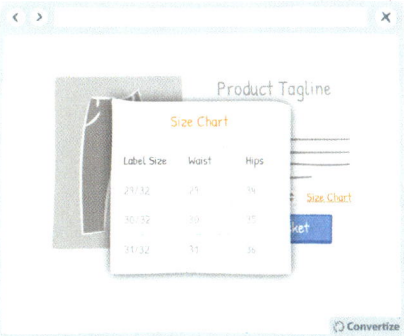

The information you provide on a product page should give a potential customer all the information they need to make a purchase. Unfortunately, the Curse of Knowledge makes it difficult to gauge how much you need to tell them and how much they already know.

For example, clothing retailers often give standard sizes in their product descriptions. This might seem like enough detail, but it does not tell customers what the corresponding dimensions are. Dresses are listed from size 6 upwards, but many people do not know how this relates to bust, waist and hip measurements. Trousers are sometimes described as S, M, L and XL without explaining how long, wide or skinny they are.

The Curse of Knowledge is one reason customers experience the Ambiguity Effect (Principle 25). To avoid losing conversions, ensure you provide enough information for anyone to make a purchase.

Sources and further examples:

Sources:
- Camerer, Loewenstein & Weber, 1989
- Newton, 1990

Further examples on this PRIVATE page:
www.smart-persuasion.com/curse-of-knowledge

Ambiguity Effect

Principle 25

(Ellsberg, 1961)

Description of the Principle:

The Ambiguity Effect describes the tendency people have to avoid options with unknown results, or about which they lack information. Decision-making is affected by a general bias against doubt and ambiguity. People tend to select options for which the outcome is more certain – even if it isn't necessarily the most advantageous outcome - because they prefer surer things. The concept is expressed in the proverb: "Better the devil you know than the devil you don't". It is therefore more likely that someone will choose to invest their time or money in an action for which they already know the outcome than in one with less certain consequences. In other words, people avoid doing things or making choices they know less about. This results in a reluctance to try new things and a limited ability to recognise the long-term benefits of riskier decisions compared to marginal gains from safer choices.

Why this Principle works:

The Ambiguity Effect was first studied by Daniel Ellsberg in 1961, when he conducted an experiment now known as the "Ellsberg Paradox". The experiment offered participants the chance to play a game in which players blindly drew a ball from a box and guess its colour to win $20. They could choose to draw the ball from one of two boxes: one contained 50 red balls and 50 green balls, whereas the second contained 100 red and green balls in an unknown proportion.

The results showed that most people preferred to choose from the 50/50 box as, even though not knowing the distribution of ball colours in the second box meant they couldn't know whether 50/50 would be a more advantageous box for guessing. They preferred to make use of the information provided - even though it didn't necessarily increase the likelihood of them winning - than to go with the more ambiguous alternative.

How to use this Principle:

The Ambiguity Effect should be taken into account when devising your marketing strategy. If a potential customer knows less about your company than they do about a competing company, they are more likely to go with your competitor. This is simply because they will prefer an option that provides more certainty. Therefore, it is important to opt for a strategy that places importance on clarity and providing enough information to ensure that the Ambiguity Effect doesn't result in lost business.

Concrete Application Example:

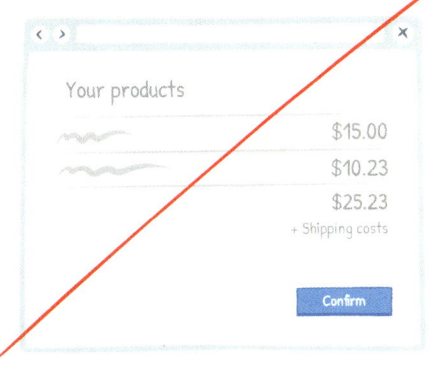 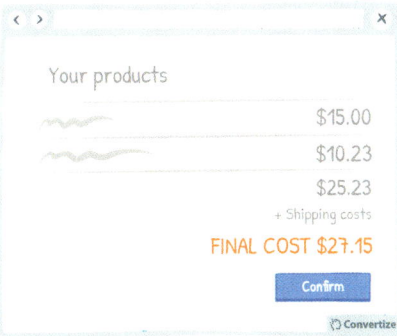

Your customers want to have all relevant payment information before completing a purchase. If they feel unsure about what they are going to be charged, they are more likely to abandon the basket before paying.

Research has shown that people avoid proceeding with actions when the results are unknown, or when they don't feel they have enough information.

By displaying the final price in the shopping basket before the checkout page is reached, you will increase the chances that your customer will complete the purchase.

Sources and further examples:

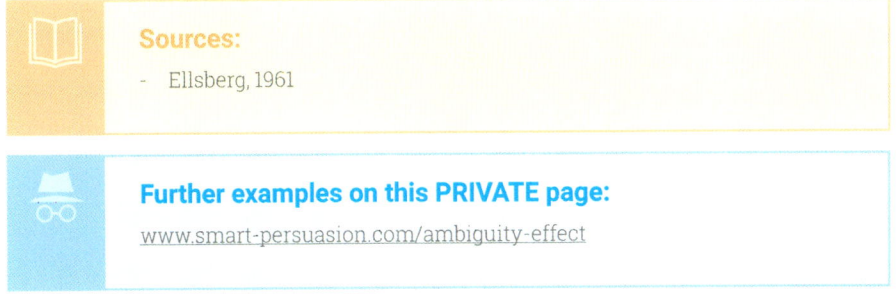

Sources:
- Ellsberg, 1961

Further examples on this PRIVATE page:
www.smart-persuasion.com/ambiguity-effect

> Principle 26

Extrinsic Motivation

(Deci, 1975; Deci & Ryan, 1985; 2002)

Description of the Principle:

The distinction between Intrinsic Motivation and Extrinsic Motivation was first looked at by Edward Deci in 1975. He later studied this subject in more detail alongside Richard M. Ryan in 1985 and 2002. They suggested that motivation can be defined according to the factors that provoke it. When motivation is induced by an external factor (reward, social pressure, approval of a third party, etc.) it is called an Extrinsic Motivation.

Inversely, Intrinsic Motivation comes from an individual internal factor such as personal interest or desire. For example, if someone exercises to clear their head and to relax, then it is due to Intrinsic Motivation.

Why this Principle works:

Depending on the context, either Intrinsic or Extrinsic Motivation can be more effective. Extrinsic Motivation is often most effective when engaging someone to complete a simple task. However, when the task is more complicated and might require more in-depth thought and creativity, this type of motivation has been found to be a hindrance. This was clearly shown during Glucksberg's experiment, which was based on Duncker's famous cognitive test "The Candle Problem". In Duncker's test, first used in 1945, participants were shown into a room where they were presented with a candle, a box of tacks and a box of matches. They were then asked to attach the candle to a cork board and light it whilst ensuring that none of the wax would fall on to the table below. The solution is to empty the tack box, put the candle inside, use the tacks to attach the box to the cork board then use the matches to light the candle.

Tests on this have overwhelmingly proven that when the person is shown the tacks already outside of their box they generally come to the right solution relatively easily, whereas when the tacks are inside their box, more lateral thinking and creativity is required. The interesting aspect to Glucksberg's version of the experiment was the difference that adding an Extrinsic Motivation to these two test groups made. Participants were split into two groups: Group A was simply asked to complete the task as quickly as possible, whilst Group B was offered the following financial reward: the person who solved it quickest would receive $150 and others who finished in the top 25% of times would receive $40.

Within these 2 groups, half were shown the simpler scenario in which the tacks were already outside the box, and the other half, the more complex scenario. Results showed that in the simpler scenario, it was in fact Group B who performed the best. The extrinsic motivational tool of the financial reward was proven to be very effective for this simpler task. However, in the more complex scenario the results were reversed as Group B found the combination of time pressure and potential financial reward to actually *limit* their ability to think creatively and find the solution.

How to use this Principle:

This principle has many implications for persuasive strategies. For digital marketing, it is important to determine which type of motivation will be the most effective in persuading your visitors to complete an action (clicking a call-to-action, for example). If the requested task is simple enough, then adding some kind of incentive or other form of Extrinsic Motivation could help to increase conversions. If the task is more complex or asks for a higher level of attention and creativity, it is better to persuade customers by highlighting their own internal motivations (such as a sense of personal accomplishment).

Concrete Application Example:

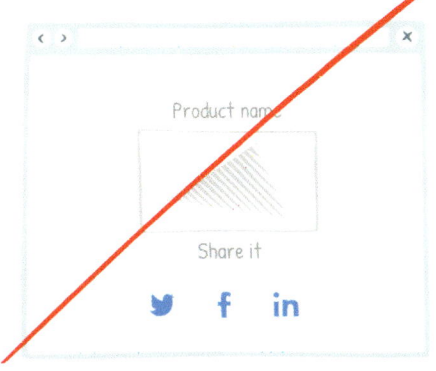 

Offering an incentive to your visitors to share your content or their purchases on social media will obviously increase the likelihood of them doing so. This incentive could be anything from offering a discount (such as the 10% shown in the image) or another tangible or symbolic reward. Studies have shown that this type of added motivation - called Extrinsic Motivation - is particularly effective in encouraging people to carry out small tasks. Providing these kinds of motivations for something simple, like a share on social media, is an effective strategy.

Sources and further examples:

Sources:
- Glucksberg, 1962
- Deci, 1975
- Deci & Ryan, 1985; 2002

Further examples on this PRIVATE page:
www.smart-persuasion.com/extrinsic-motivation

Principle 27

Cognitive Friction

(Sweller, 1988)

Description of the Principle:

Cognitive Friction theory, developed by John Sweller (1988), refers to the total amount of mental effort being used in the working memory. Sweller described the process as having three main stages: sensory memory, working memory and long-term memory. Your sensory memory receives all the information from your daily actions and activities (sounds, smells and everything you see). Then that sensory information passes into your working memory which either processes or discards it. If your brain processes the information, tries to categorise it, learn it, or put it in a "knowledge structure/schema", then this information passes into long-term memory. Once this has taken place, we begin to process the information automatically and without much cognitive effort.

Why this Principle works:

Cognitive Friction theory is based on the fact that individuals are limited in their working memory capacity, and thus understand and learn more easily through instructional methods that avoid overloading it with superfluous information. In other words, heavy cognitive load can have a negative effect on task completion, and leads to further errors and interference in the task. Learning happens best under conditions that are aligned with this human cognitive architecture.

For example, studies have shown that the widespread use of laptops and cell phones in classrooms has generally reduced academic success. Indeed, it increases the distractions available for students (who will inevitably check Facebook and emails whilst also taking part in the class) which in turn increases their overall cognitive load. This ultimately reduces the space available in the working memory for effective reception of important information.

How to use this Principle:

Cognitive Friction theory has many applications in web marketing, especially with the continuous development of new technologies. Some navigation functions risk overloading users and driving them into a state of cognitive strain, which then lessens the likelihood of them taking desirable actions such as filling in a form or completing a purchase.

Concrete Application Example:

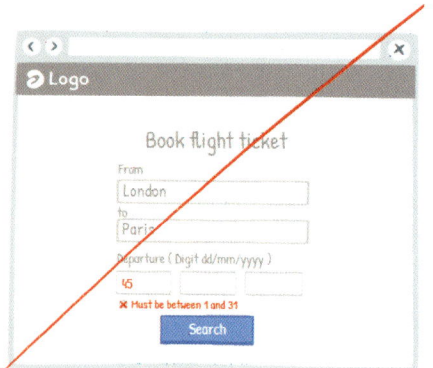
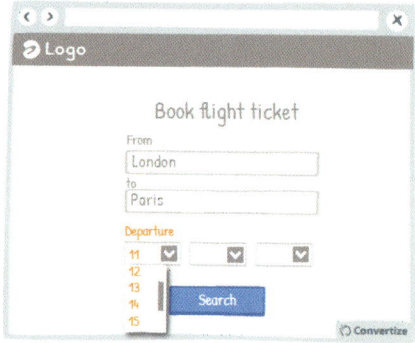

In order to avoid preventable errors and possible frustration on the part of your customer, don't give them the ability to enter incorrect information. For example, as in the above drawing, when someone is required to input a date, make sure they can only select from a list of relevant information. This will make user experience much clearer and more intuitive, and the easier and more pleasant your customer finds your site to use, the more likely they will be to convert.

Sources and further examples:

Sources:
- Sweller, 1988

Further examples on this PRIVATE page:
www.smart-persuasion.com/cognitive-friction

Motivating Uncertainty Effect

Principle 28

(Skinner, 1950; Moon & Nelson, 2014; Klein & Fishbach, 2014)

Description of the Principle:

Historical research has shown how people tend to avoid risk or ambiguity (eg. Ambiguity Aversion, Ellsberg, 1961; Risk Aversion, Tversky & Kahneman, 1979). However, more recent research (Moon & Nelson; Klein & Fishbach, 2014) has begun to suggest that uncertain rewards can actually be a strong motivator for completing a task. This is known as the Motivating-Uncertainty Effect. For example, imagine a competition where a task must be completed to win a monetary prize. In Scenario A the prize total is fixed at a moderate amount. In Scenario B it is unknown (it could be very small or very large). People are more likely to be motivated by the competition in Scenario B.

Researchers have found that this system of variable rewards makes the experience more exciting as we are stimulated by the unknown. This means we will be more motivated to complete a task where the reward is variable.

Why this Principle works:

This principle can also lead people to have more interest in repetitive tasks. In the 1950s, the psychologist B. F. Skinner conducted a well-known experiment called "The Skinner Box". During this experiment, Skinner observed that lab mice responded most strongly to random rewards. The mice were presented with a lever to press, and a random outcome followed each time they did. Sometimes they would receive a small treat, sometimes a large treat, and sometimes nothing at all. The mice were shown to press the lever compulsively, becoming addicted to the unknown pattern of rewards.

In 2014, a similar experiment was carried out using people. Participants were asked to drink a large quantity of water in 2 minutes. Group A was told that they would receive a reward of 2 dollars for completing this task and Group B was told that they would receive either 1 or 2 dollars. The results showed that 70% of Group B (with the variable reward) completed the task as opposed to 43% of Group A.

How to use this Principle:

The Motivating-Uncertainty Effect can be used effectively in business and marketing. Offering uncertain rewards can be a powerful strategy for gaining and maintaining customer loyalty. For example, it is easier to encourage an online visitor to complete a desired action (buy, click, share, sign up, etc.) if this comes with an unknown reward.

Concrete Application Example:

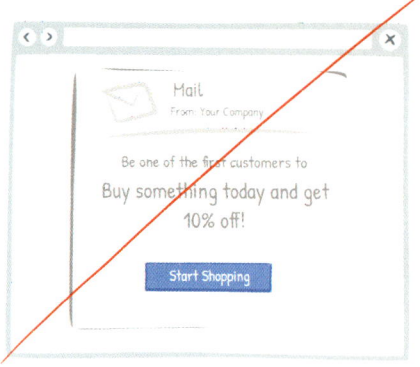 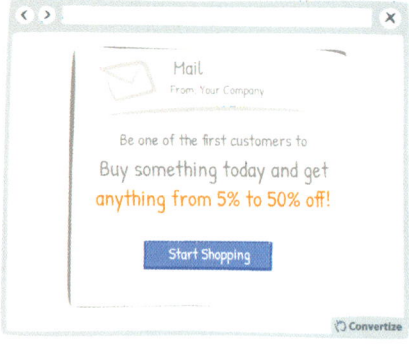

If using an incentive to encourage visitors to your website to take an action like providing their email, it is better to provide a mystery reward than a clearly defined one. The user will be intrigued by the unknown aspect of the task, and is more likely to be motivated to provide their email address than if the reward is obvious, like an eBook or a discount. This is because people want to resolve uncertainty where they encounter it.

Sources and further examples:

Sources:
- Skinner, 1950
- Moon & Nelson, 2014
- Klein & Fishbach, 2014

Further examples on this PRIVATE page:
www.smart-persuasion.com/motivating-uncertainty-effect

Principle 29

Choice-Supportive Bias

(Henkel & Mather, 2007)

Description of the Principle:

In cognitive science, Choice-Supportive Bias is the tendency to remember our choices as better than they actually were. This is because we tend to over attribute positive features to options we chose and negative features to options we did not choose. Individuals tend to think that because they chose an option it must have been the better one. As a result we feel good about ourselves and our choices, and have less regret for bad decisions.

Why this Principle works:

For example, Henkel & Mather (2007) conducted an experiment based on participants' choices over a number of sessions. They found that giving people false reminders about an option they had previously chosen led them to remember that choice as the best one. In the first session, participants had to decide between two used cars, each with a list of features (such as a radio, new tyres, air conditioning). In the second session, Henkel and Mather gave them a new list of features for each of the two options. Some new positive and negative features had been mixed in with the old ones. Next, participants were asked to indicate whether each feature (such as power steering) was new, had been associated with the option they chose, or had been associated with the option they rejected.

Participants attributed the most positive features to the option they had originally chosen, even those that were completely new and hadn't been attributed to either car in the first session.

How to use this Principle:

Choice-Supportive Bias has applications in digital marketing. You can use it to get your customers to attribute positive features to your brand and products, and even negative ones to others. One strategy could be to show previously visited pages and bought items to your visitors (in other words remind them that they have already "chosen" you). Another good practice can be reassuring customers on the choices they make to enhance their own Choice-Supportive Bias and result in greater post-purchase satisfaction.

Concrete Application Example:

 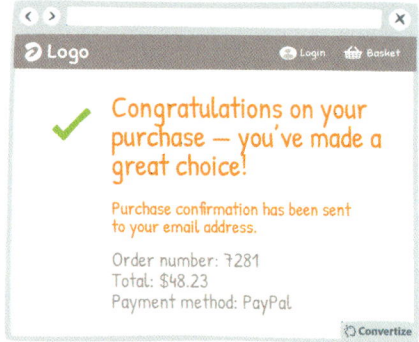

Don't hesitate to congratulate your customers on their purchases. This repeated affirmation that they are making a good choice will cement feelings of positivity and satisfaction around their purchase. Furthermore, it will lead to more post-purchase satisfaction. Indeed, we tend to remember our choices as being good ones, as we like to convince ourselves that we have behaved correctly. Reinforcing this pre-disposition with affirmative messages and praise, which can be awarded to customers throughout the conversional funnel and in a post-purchase email, will ensure a higher post-purchase satisfaction and customer loyalty.

Sources and further examples:

Sources:
- Henkel & Mather, 2000

Further examples on this PRIVATE page:
www.smart-persuasion.com/choice-supportive-bias

Principle 30

Paradox of Choice

(Schwartz, 2004)

Description of the Principle:

The Paradox of Choice principle is explored by the American psychologist Barry Schwartz in his book *The Paradox of Choice – Why More Is Less* (2004). Schwartz shows how, instead of increasing our capacity to make a decision, an abundance of choice can often lead to feelings of anxiety, loneliness and depression. Even if we might think we'd be happier if given a larger range of choices, we actually make better decisions and end up happier and more satisfied when fewer options are presented to us.

Having fewer choices results in reduced consumer anxiety, as too many options can be overwhelming. Choosing just one from a large selection of desirable options can lead us to feel dissatisfied, as we become hung up on those other possibilities we missed out on. The more choices we are given, the higher our expectations become and the lower our eventual sense of accomplishment and satisfaction. It can even lead to "suspended action": where we are so overwhelmed by the choice on offer that we fail to make a decision at all.

Why this Principle works:

This sensation should be familiar. Ever been on one of those Christmas shopping trips where you wander aimlessly without a set idea of what you need to buy? You usually end up not buying anything, having spent the whole time deliberating. Or, when you want to watch a movie with someone and you're both sat in front of the TV, scrolling endlessly through a video streaming service like Netflix. Even when you narrow down your choice by selecting a category, and are both able to discount some films that you've already seen, there are still dozens of options available. Not only do you not want to invest time in a bad movie, but you also don't want to unwittingly miss a better one, so you keep searching. You may even give up, deciding against watching a movie because the abundance of choice makes the decision too difficult!

How to use this Principle:

The Paradox of Choice is often applied in the world of sales and marketing, as it can greatly affect consumer purchase decisions. Whether shopping in store or online, customers can often be put off making that final purchase if shown too many products or if too much cognitive effort is required of them to make a decision. Under this cognitive pressure, customers will tend to either forgo making a purchase, or make a decision that will ultimately leave them feeling dissatisfied. It's therefore incredibly important to ensure that it is simple for your customers to make a choice, so that they don't feel overwhelmed and so their final decision is satisfactory for both them and you.

Concrete Application Example:

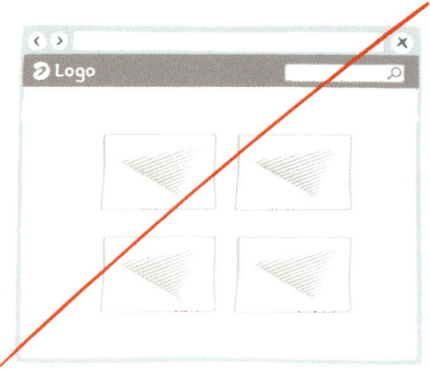
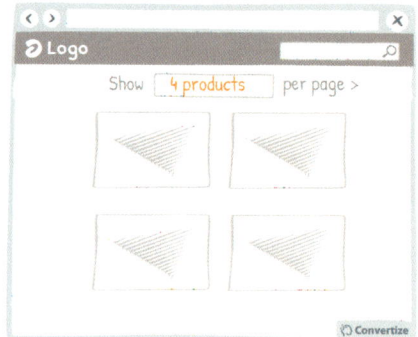

Adding an option to adjust the number of items displayed per page allows your visitor to feel more in control of how they spend time on your site. This will also allow them to adjust the layout to what they are most comfortable with. The more at ease they feel, the more trust they will place in your brand and products. Moreover, giving an option to reduce the number of products shown often leads to more satisfying decision-making.

Research has demonstrated that information overload leads individuals to reach less effective and satisfactory decisions than they would with less information or fewer options.

It is helpful to provide multiple different filter options. However, be careful not to overdo this and set a default option - you don't want your customers to feel overwhelmed by too many filter choices, too!

Sources and further examples:

Sources:
- Schwartz, 2004

Further examples on this PRIVATE page:
www.smart-persuasion.com/paradox-of-choice

Principle 31

Foot-in-the-door Technique

(Freedman & Fraser, 1966)

Description of the Principle:

The Foot-in-the-door Technique is the idea that it is more effective to start by asking people for something small, and then when they give it to you, you are in a better position to ask for something bigger. Indeed, Freedman and Fraser (1966) have shown that a small agreement creates a bond between the requester and the requestee. The person you ask acts according to the cognitive bias that they have to justify their agreement to themselves. Humans like to believe they have made all the right decisions, so they will convince themselves that they accepted the first request for a good reason. They will then feel obliged to act consistently with this reason by accepting a second and third request, and so on.

The phrase "foot in the door" originated during the heyday of door-to-door salespeople who would place their foot in the way of a closing door. With their foot literally in the door, the potential customer would have to listen to the sales pitch and this would potentially give them their way in.

Why this Principle works:

Freedman and Fraser conducted many studies that demonstrated this cognitive bias. In one of them, they asked people to place either a small sign in their car window to promote safe driving, or a small sign in a window of their house about keeping California clean. About two weeks later, the same people were asked by a second person to put a large sign advocating safe driving or "keeping California clean" in their front garden. Many people who agreed to the first request also complied with the second, far more intrusive request.

How to use this Principle:

The Foot-in-the-door Technique also works as a digital marketing strategy. For example, you can begin by asking someone for seemingly unimportant information, such as their postcode or age (this should be a small request that doesn't cost anything, isn't intrusive and doesn't take too much time). Once the person has given this, they are more likely to agree to a larger request, such as registering online or signing up for a newsletter.

Concrete Application Example:

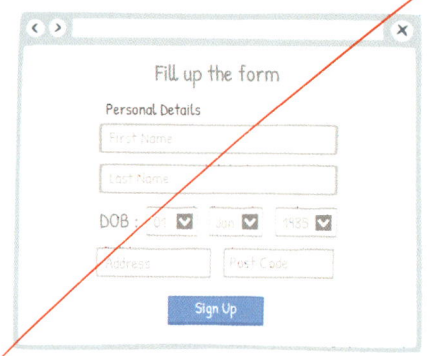 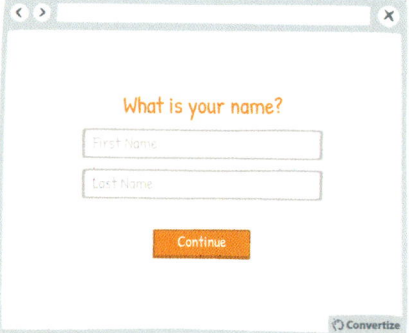

Making a form easy and fun to fill in will encourage people to complete it and convert. Starting your form by asking for a lot of personal information will annoy people and they are more likely to abandon the signup process.

Asking a simple question at first will help people become engaged and complete the form. You could ask them an easy question related to the registration process, such as: "How big is your team?" After they've done this you can move them on to the next stage of the form. As they've already become engaged, they are more likely to complete the process and convert.

Sources and further examples:

Sources:
- Freedman & Fraser, 1966

Further examples on this PRIVATE page:

www.smart-persuasion.com/foot-in-the-door-technique-fitd

Intention & Self-Regulation

Principle 32

(Gollwitzer, 1993;1999)

Description of the Principle:

Intention and Self-Regulation, first studied by Gollwitzer in 1993, suggests that planning how you will reach a certain goal will increase your chances of reaching it. In fact, Gollwitzer found it can double (or even triple) your chances of succeeding. Gollwitzer describes this as an "implementation intention", a self-regulatory stategy which follows this set wording: "If (such and such occurs) then (I will take the following steps...)". Framing your intention into this "if - then" formula makes you more likely to achieve it than simply relying on your motivation and desire. For example, we may be highly motivated to get rid of our bad habits or alter a certain behavioural pattern but still find it difficult to initiate these changes or indeed to maintain them.

Setting a precise intention or plan greatly increases the likelihood that you will act upon your motivations. This is because they are now connected to something precise, such as a deadline or an activity, increasing their tangibility and creating future triggers. You already have the mental representation of your future actions available to you ,which makes it much easier to actually carry them out. This type of implementation intention is particularly effective when used for long-term goals that can be difficult to get started on (such as losing weight, changing your diet, passing your exams or renovating your house).

Why this Principle works:

Several scientific experiments have proven the success of this Intention and Self-Regulation strategy. One of these, published in the *British Journal of Health Psychology*, studied the frequency with which three groups of participants (chosen at random with no criteria for initial physical health) exercised over a period of two weeks. Each group was given different instructions before starting: Group A (witness group) was given a random text to read (not to do with sporting activity at all) and told to keep track of any exercise they did over the 2 week period. Group B (motivation group) was given a text on the benefits of sport and the dangers of not exercising regularly and then asked to keep track of their exercise levels the same as Group A. Group C (intention group) was not only given the same text as Group B to read but was also asked to say out loud how often they intended to exercise over the following 2 weeks.

The results showed that 91% of Group C (the intention group) exercised at least once each week, in contrast to 35% of Group B and 38% of Group A. This suggests that motivatation is not a strong predictor of success. However, setting a solid intention will give you the best chance of carrying out an objective.

How to use this Principle:

This principle has numerous professional applications, whether to help your business reach certain goals or indeed to encourage customers to act (or react) in a certain way. For example, to encourage people to achieve their fitness goals, you could provide them with a clear set of instructions (like a list of exercise regimes for them to follow).

Concrete Application Example:

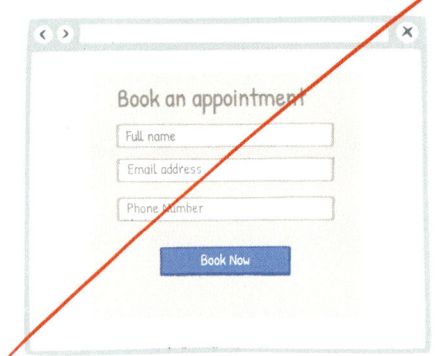 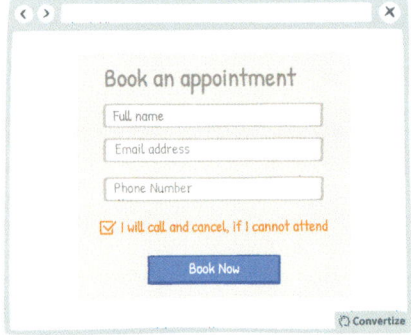

In several studies Dan Ariely has shown that if patients are asked to confirm that they will call and cancel if they cannot attend, they are not only more likely to do so but also less likely to miss their appointment. A simple opt-in box added to your booking page could be enough to regulate attendance and prevent cancelations.

Sources and further examples:

Sources:
- Gollwitzer, 1993; 1999

Further examples on this PRIVATE page:

www.smart-persuasion.com/intention-and-self-regulation

Principle 33

Autonomy Bias

(Deci, 1971; Ryan, 2008)

Description of the Principle:

The Autonomy Bias is part of the theory of Self-Determination studied by Deci (1971) and Ryan (2008), which explores the degree to which an individual's behaviour is self-motivated. Autonomy Bias is our universal and innate need to be agents of our own lives. We have a need to make our own choices and to have the ability to implement these choices by our own free will. This includes deciding what we do, how we do it, when we do it and where we do it. A high level of perceived autonomy comes with feelings of certainty, reduced stress and a high level of 'Intrinsic Motivation'. These all increase the likelihood of persistent behaviour. We especially don't like to feel coerced: it undermines this Intrinsic Motivation and we become less interested in doing something.

Why this Principle works:

Studies have shown that restrictions on our autonomy lead to dissatisfaction. For example, one study revealed that the greatest source of dissatisfaction amongst doctors wasn't having to deal with insurance companies or the piles of paperwork but rather a lack of control over their daily schedules.

Studies also show that even altruistic actions (normally shown to increase positivity and well-being) will fail to produce these positive feelings when they're coerced.

How to use this Principle:

Autonomy Bias has applications in management and marketing. It can be a tool for motivating employees or customers to get the best response and engagement from them by knowing when and how best to award them autonomy.

Concrete Application Example:

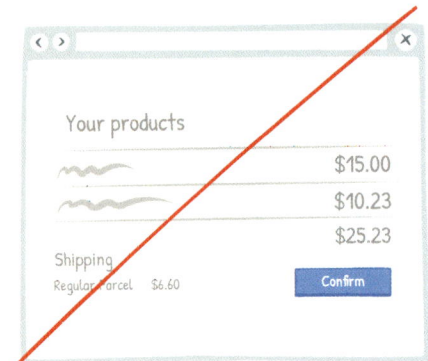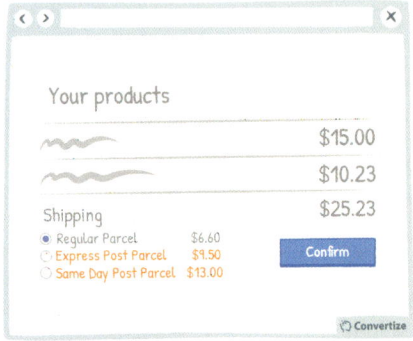

Offering multiple delivery options is important both to offer choice to the customer but also for the possibility of further profit made on that purchase. Customers like to have a sense of control over their purchasing and different delivery options are always appreciated. Research has shown that we are drawn towards immediate gratification and so the possibility of quicker delivery time may be the factor that encourages them to complete their purchase. It will also add another profitable element onto the purchase for you.

Sources and further examples:

Having vs Using Effect

Principle 34

(Kahn & Meyer, 1991; Mukherjee & Hoyer, 2001;
Hamilton & Thompson, 2007; Goodman & Irmak, 2012)

Description of the Principle:

The Having vs Using Effect has been observed by many different researchers, amongst them Goodman & Irmak (2012). Their studies have shown that people tend to prefer (and will pay more for) products and services that come with multiple features, even if they are unlikely to actually use them.

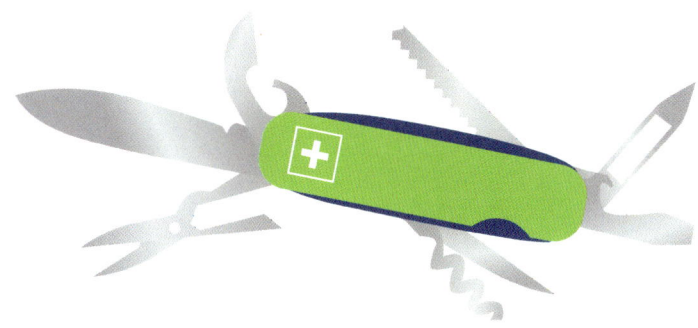

For example, we are more drawn towards subscription tariffs (phone contracts, travel cards, etc.) than pay-per-use models, even though it could actually work out cheaper for us in the long run. Equally, we are drawn towards something with the largest number of, or most up-to-date, features, often without fully considering the likelihood that we will actually use these features.

Why this Principle works:

Goodman & Irmak discovered a number of reasons behind the Having vs Using Effect. The more complex and technical the functions of a product, or the less familiar they are to us, the more we are at risk of falling victim to the Having vs Using Effect. This is because we struggle to effectively evaluate how much we will use particular features, and therefore how much value to place on them. We're also likely to think that a product with more features must be a better product, simply because it has something that another product doesn't, and so are willing to pay more for it. We are prone to think more in terms of what we are going to "have" (the overall product, which is perceived to be a better one) than what we will realistically "use". This cognitive bias stems from the fashionability of consumerism, whereby we buy the latest upgraded models simply for the social status they bring, and regardless of whether we will make full use of any additional features.

How to use this Principle:

Studies have shown that in a situation in which we are forced to think about our actual usage of an item, we often pick different products. Putting aside the number of functions available and picking a product based on our own individual requirements typically results in a more satisfying purchase. In the commercial world, the Having vs Using Effect is often used to sell new and function-heavy items - that are generally much more expensive - by presenting these items to customers in terms of what they could "have" rather than what they will actually "use". This encourages customers to think of the product in its totality, rather than as a collection of individual uses.

Concrete Application Example:

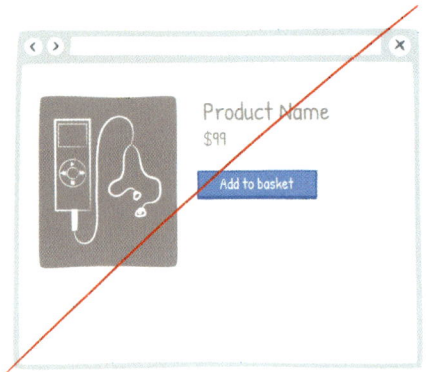 

On your product page, it is best to list all available features rather than just choosing to display a few of the main ones. People are generally more drawn towards products with lots of features and will find a long list clearly displaying everything they will get more persuasive.

When we are choosing which products to buy, or deciding whether to upgrade to a newer model, we often concentrate on what we will have rather than what we will actually use.

So it doesn't matter if only 3 of the features are the ones most people will really make use of, the more features you can let people know they will have, the more likely they will be to desire the product.

Sources and further examples:

Sources:
- Kahn & Meyer, 1991
- Mukherjee & Hoyer, 2001
- Hamilton & Thompson, 2007
- Goodman & Irmak, 2012

Further examples on this PRIVATE page:
www.smart-persuasion.com/having-vs-using-effect

Scarcity

Principle 35

(Worchel, Lee & Adewole, 1975)

Description of the Principle:

The Scarcity Principle was discovered by scientists Worchel, Lee and Adewole in 1975. They conducted an experiment simply using a jar full of cookies, and another jar that was almost empty. They found that people overwhelmingly desired a cookie from the jar that was almost empty simply because it was scarce. This effect also creates a sense of urgency, as people want to get the scarce product before it is gone entirely.

Why this Principle works:

This principle is explained by the idea that the more difficult or urgent it is to acquire an item, or the more easily it might be lost, the more value that item has in our minds. Scarcity is associated in our brains with something positive, luxurious and exclusive. We automatically assume that something is scarce because everyone wants or has already bought this product. Therefore, it must be a good product. In other words, scarce objects pique our interest, becoming more desirable than a product that is readily available.

How to use this Principle:

Many brands make use of this principle through the way they market their products. By offering limited edition products, flash sales, or only producing something in limited supply, brands are able to stimulate demand. For example, just one day after Apple launched the latest iPhone, stocks had already sold out. This made even more people want to buy it because it seemed scarce, even though new stocks became available very quickly.

Concrete Application Example:

"Fear of Missing Out" (Principle 44) is by now a well-known concept. Utilising this to its full potential can enable you to have more efficient and meaningful interactions with your clients: nudging them to buy, book or subscribe.

One way to act on this principle is to add information about the quantity remaining, such as the notification 'only 4 left in stock'.

Sources and further examples:

Sources:
- Worchel, Lee & Adewole, 1975

Further examples on this PRIVATE page:
www.smart-persuasion.com/scarcity

Commitment & Consistency

Principle 36

(Cialdini, 1984)

Description of the Principle:

The Commitment and Consistency principle is one of the six Principles of Persuasion established by Robert Cialdini (1984) in his book *Influence: The Psychology of Persuasion*. It describes the way in which people want their beliefs and behaviours to be consistent with their values and self-image. Firstly, we tend to view consistency as an attractive social trait and as indicative of someone being rational, trustworthy and stable. Secondly, the Commitment and Consistency principle is a mental shortcut we use: we simplify the many choices we face by using past decisions as reference for related choices. The consequence of this cognitive bias is that we act in ways that are consistent with our initial action or thought, so that when we commit to something or someone, we stick to it. We also try to behave in ways that are consistent with the image we have portrayed to others, and with the public image they have of us.

Why this Principle works:

For example, if an individual is thought of as someone who knows about politics, he or she is more likely to participate in subsequent political conversations, even if they lack knowledge of that topic. This is due to wanting to remain consistent with the public perception of their character. In the same way, children who are often congratulated by their parents for achievements and working hard are more likely to continue to work hard and do well in order to remain consistent with this external perception of themselves.

How to use this Principle:

The Commitment and Consistency principle is important to consider when deciding your marketing strategy. Encouraging customers to make a small commitment to your brand or site (by asking them to complete an easy task or offering them something for free) puts you in a better position to motivate them to continue engaging with your site. They will feel compelled to remain consistent with this initial behaviour.

Concrete Application Example:

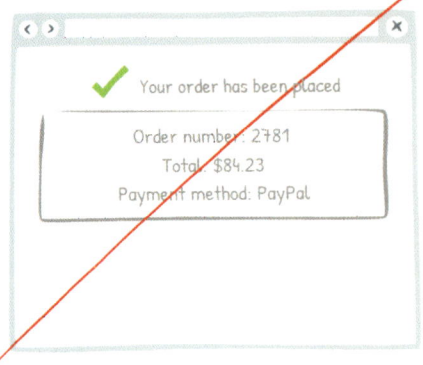 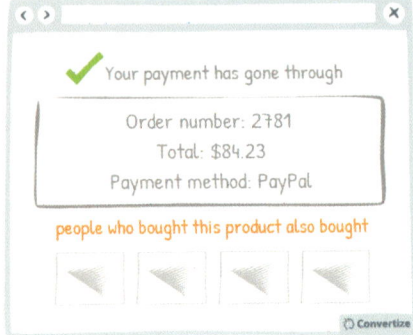

On the confirmation page after purchase, display "people who bought this product also bought ..." to create a double funnel. This will encourage your customers to make a second purchase after completing the first. Indeed, people are more likely to make another purchase if they have already completed one, as we like to stay consistent with our own actions.

We also tend to be swayed by the decisions of others and so showing visitors what other customers have purchased can be highly influential. Displaying this on the confirmation page means you can achieve an upsell without distracting customers from completing their original purchase. Even if the customer doesn't make any of the additional suggested purchases immediately, this will still give them ideas of products to buy in the weeks or months ahead, increasing the average basket amount.

Sources and further examples:

Sources:
- Worchel, Lee & Adewole, 1975
- Cialdini, 1984

Further examples on this PRIVATE page:
www.smart-persuasion.com/commitment-and-consistency

Metaphor Effect

Principle 37

(Lakoff & Johnson, 1980)

Description of the Principle:

The Metaphor Effect describes the way in which our brains react to metaphors. These are language formulas that describe something by likening it to an associated image. To have "a heart of stone" is one such metaphor, in which the stone represents a hard and cold element, qualities that translate as lacking feeling or empathy when applied to the heart. The Metaphor Effect describes the way in which we tend to understand and remember metaphorical language more easily, as it activates our imagination.

Metaphors engage the right hemisphere of the brain, which controls our mental imagery (the same function that allows us to dream). The images created are more easily understood and more memorable than simple literal language. The senses and emotions are activated by metaphorical language, going beyond the literal sense of a phrase into the realm of imagery and more abstract concepts. Like all analogies, metaphors help us to understand more complex ideas and enrich the language we use.

Harness the power of Zeus!

Why this Principle works:

Metaphorical language is therefore a compelling form of communication that allows you, in certain cases, to better convey your message. If a metaphor can help transmit imagery and emotion, your reader is more likely to notice and retain the information it conveys. This is because people are much more likely to connect and engage with something that touches them emotionally.

How to use this Principle:

In digital marketing, the use of metaphors can greatly help to improve the quality of content on your site. When we're on the internet, our senses are less stimulated than they would be when browsing a physical store. Using metaphorical language can help to stimulate a wider range of senses and emotions. This is especially important when attempting to convey more abstract ideas.

The Metaphor Effect is particularly persuasive as it engages a customer's imagination and intuition, which are much more receptive to new ideas than analytical faculties.

Concrete Application Example:

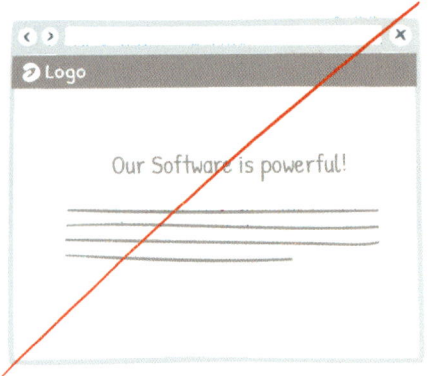

Metaphorical language can help you to attract attention from potential customers and make it easier for them to retain information about your products. Further, by engaging your customers with unexpected and emotive images, you can ensure they are more open to new ideas and persuasion, encouraging them to act.

When describing a product, avoid unfounded or generic claims. These are likely to be discarded as a simple sales pitch. Instead, provide evidence for your product's quality with facts and testimonials. If this evidence is not available, or if you are highlighting an attribute that is not easy to explain (such as an experience or a technical feature) use helpful images instead.

The Metaphor Effect is particularly useful when building up a brand. Using an image to communicate your Value Proposition (the tactic adopted by Amazon, an eCommerce and delivery service designed to be the world's largest and fastest) will make it both memorable and persuasive.

Sources and further examples:

Sources:
- Lakoff & Johnson, 1980

Further examples on this PRIVATE page:
www.smart-persuasion.com/metaphor-effect

Principle 38

Psychological Reactance

(Brehm, 1966)

Description of the Principle:

Psychological Reactance is a cognitive bias that was initially studied by Jack Brehm in 1966. It describes the extreme reactions we experience when we feel pushed towards doing something, or when we feel as though our freedom to make choices is threatened. Reactance is a psychological defence mechanism that we utilise more or less subconsciously in order to try and get back our freedom. We become "motivationally aroused", meaning we're flooded with an excess of righteous motivation that leads us to fight for those freedoms. This often manifests itself as non-conformity, meaning we end up supporting the very position or behaviour that we were being pushed away from. In other words, when we feel we are being forced into something, we often end up with a very negative perception of whatever that is and consequently tend to do the exact opposite. Research has shown that the more we feel our freedom of choice is being threatened, the more extreme our reactance will be.

Why this Principle works:

Kiesler, Mathog, Pool & Howenstine conducted an experiment by contacting two groups of young women and asking them to sign a petition for opening a family planning and contraception clinic. One of these groups was then also sent some anti-contraception propaganda. The experiment revealed that many more of the women from the group who had also received this anti-contraception propaganda signed the petition supporting the family planning and contraception clinic than from the group that had not. Instead of inciting a negative reaction against contraception as the propaganda had intended, it had in fact had the opposite result, encouraging the women to support the contrasting cause.

How to use this Principle:

An awareness of Psychological Reactance can be effective for persuasive strategies, especially in marketing, to encourage a certain behaviour or reaction from your customers. However, it is more important to be aware of the effect as something to avoid. Overly coercive marketing strategies, or biased promotional content, often produces the opposite effect to the one intended.

Concrete Application Example:

 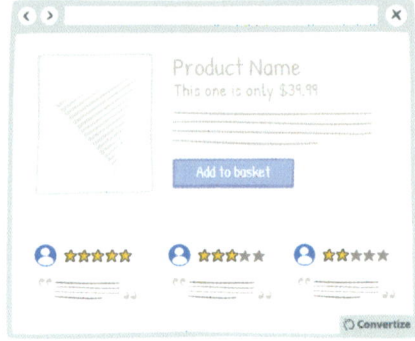

Some websites hide negative reviews or drawbacks. Others, however, such as Amazon, display them clearly alongside the positive responses. Believe it or not, hiding your drawbacks is not the solution. Your customers will go in search for reviews about your product on other websites, or simply won't trust you because you don't seem impartial.

However, you can also use your drawbacks to show your benefits. For example, you can respond to negative reviews and say, "we don't have this option X because we have chosen to focus on this Y option to best meet your needs." This could diminish the effect of Psychological Reactance, as users won't be exposed to pushy marketing material. Instead, they will see a balanced discussion of your product's merits.

Sources and further examples:

Sources:
- Brehm, 1966
- Kiesler, Mathog, Pool & Howenstine, 1971

Further examples on this PRIVATE page:
www.smart-persuasion.com/psychological-reactance

Principle 39

Immediacy Effect

(Ainslie, 1975; Laibson, 1997; Bickel, Odum & Madden, 1999; Frederick, Loewenstein & O'Donoghue, 2002)

Description of the Principle:

The Immediacy Effect (also called "Hyperbolic Discounting" or "Present Focus Bias") is a psychological mechanism that makes people prefer an instant reward over receiving something of potentially more value in the future. This devaluing of a delayed reward leads us to prioritise immediate gratification. Our brains are wired to prefer the instant and immediate over the distant and hypothetical. Thus, instant rewards are valued more highly than future ones.

Scientists who have explored this subject have found that the Immediacy Effect is hyperbolic, meaning that it is not consistent relative to the amount of time involved. The value placed on something changes rapidly and inconsistently depending on the time delay.

Imagine you can choose between receiving an ice cream right now (Scenario A) or receiving two in a month's time (Scenario B). Most people prefer the readily available ice cream (instead of waiting a month for an additional one).

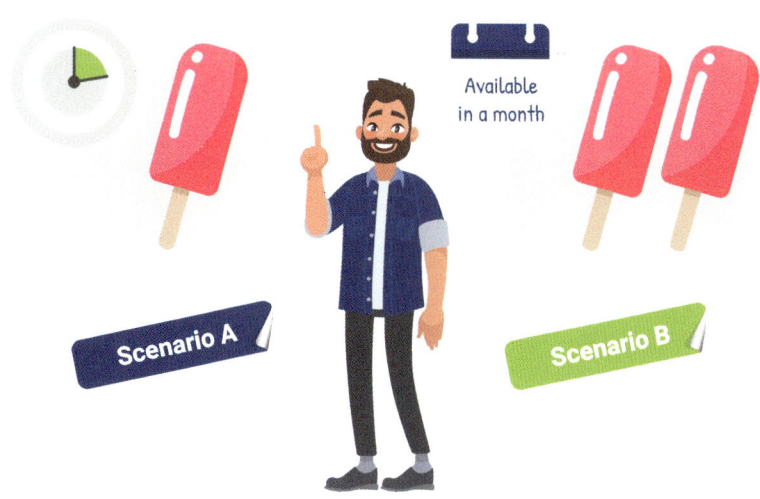

However, if we update the scenarios so that you can choose between waiting 12 months to get an ice cream (Scenario C), and 13 months to get two (Scenario D), most people will prefer to wait an extra month.

Why this Principle works:

If you were offered the choice of $100 right now or $150 in one year, you would probably choose the former. For most people, the importance of this extra $50 quickly diminishes as the delay increases. The same principle explains why we have so much trouble quitting unhealthy habits that provide us with short-term pleasure but long-term problems.

How to use this Principle:

The Immediacy Effect is important within the commercial world, as the desire to have something immediately can affect product sales. For example, delivery delays are likely to affect a customer's decision to purchase from you. On the other hand, offering express delivery will often motivate people to make a purchase, and they may be willing to pay more for it or extra for a special delivery time.

Concrete Application Example:

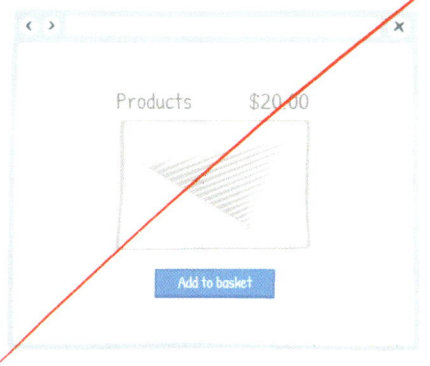 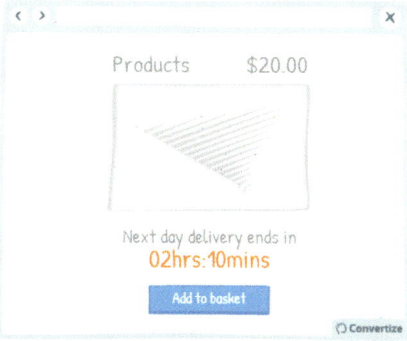

Add a countdown timer to show customers how much time they have left to make a purchase that can be delivered at the earliest possible time. People place more value on what they can access sooner. Not only would this timer harness the Immediacy Effect by making your products more desirable, but it would apply this effect earlier in the sales funnel. If you only display the quickest delivery option at the checkout, some customers may not get that far and won't experience the effect.

Sources and further examples:

Sources:
- Ainslie, 1975; Laibson, 1997
- Bickel, Odum & Madden, 1999
- Frederick, Loewenstein & O'Donoghue, 2002

Further examples on this PRIVATE page:
www.smart-persuasion.com/immediacy-effect

Principle 40

Information Bias

(Baron, Beattie & Hershey, 1988)

Description of the Principle:

Information Bias, studied by Baron, Beattie and Hershey (1988), is the tendency to believe that the more information we acquire before making a decision, the better that decision will be - even if that extra information is irrelevant.

Green Long Sleeve Shirt

Size	: Medium Regular Fit
Colour	: Green
Material	: 100% Cotton
Description	: Machine washable Stylish long sleeve shirt for fashionable men
Origin	: London
Designer	: Tom Ford
Delivery Info	: Next Day delivery available

Why this Principle works:

Baron, Beattie and Hershey demonstrated this principle with an experiment in which they gave subjects a diagnostic problem involving fictitious symptoms, tests and diseases. The majority of test subjects decided they needed to continue gathering more information and carrying out extra tests in order to make a diagnosis when in fact they had already been given sufficient data to do so.

How to use this Principle:

Information Bias can be applied to digital marketing to help encourage customers to pay specific attention to something or to make a certain choice. For example, the more information that you provide for a product, even if some of it seems irrelevant, the more likely that people will feel assured enough to make a purchase.

However, it is important to remember that any marketing content must be high quality - you shouldn't include completely unnecessary information, as it is likely to distract from your ultimate conversion goal.

Concrete Application Example:

The more information you provide on a product, the more confident customers will feel in their decision to purchase. However, too much information could ultimately distract from the product you are trying to sell.

In order to get this balance right, include a 'More info' option in the product information section. This allows customers to access more information if they require it, but lets customers satisfied with what they have already read move quickly on to the basket page.

Sources and further examples:

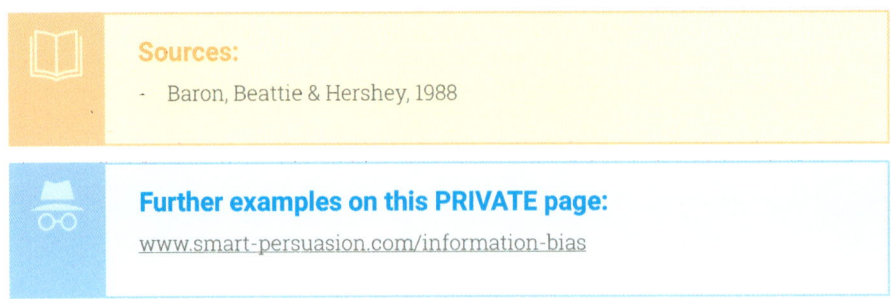

Pain of Paying

Principle 41

(Prelec & Loewenstein, 1998)

Description of the Principle:

The Pain of Paying principle, first explored by Prelec & Loewenstein in 1998, explains the psychological discomfort we experience when making a payment. Simply put, people don't like to part with their money, so making a payment can reduce the pleasure derived from acquiring a product. It has been proven that spending money actually activates the areas in our brain that are associated with physical pain and feelings of disgust.

Why this Principle works:

The more strongly we feel this "pain" when we spend money on something, the less we will enjoy buying it. This can affect the likelihood that someone will complete the final stages of a purchase. Studies have shown that certain forms of payment hurt more than others: the more evident, tangible or transparent the payment is, the less we are able to enjoy our purchase. We feel the Pain of Paying less when we pay by credit card, or when there is a distinct gap between paying and the time of receiving or using the purchase. By contrast, we feel it more when we have to pay for something immediately or by cash, as it emphasises what it is costing us.

How to use this Principle:

Allowing a quick or even a one-click payment by creating an account and storing your details is one way in which some websites reduce the Pain of Paying. Registering your customers' payment details is an effective way of limiting the feeling of making a payment and encouraging more purchases. For example, when you buy music or a movie on iTunes, there is no mention of the fact that you are paying. You simply click on the "download" button and, as your bank details are already registered, payment is automatic. This makes the process less tangible, reducing the discomfort you experience.

Concrete Application Example:

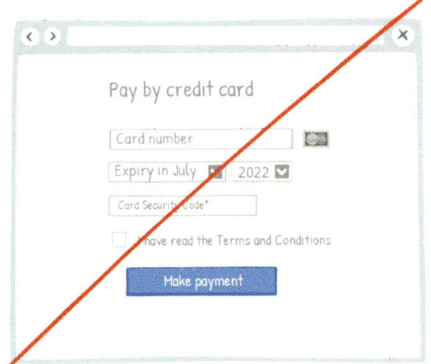 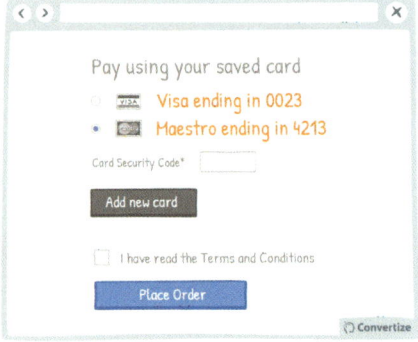

It is important to optimise the payment process as much as possible. Studies have shown that certain forms of payment 'hurt' more than others - the more observable, tangible or transparent the payment is, the less we feel the pleasure of our purchase.

Therefore, you should offer customers an easy way to renew subscriptions or make regular purchases. Saving your customers' details, so that they don't need to re-enter them for each transaction, will reduce the Pain of Paying. Your customers will be happier and more likely to buy from you again.

Sources and further examples:

Sources:
- Prelec & Loewenstein, 1998

Further examples on this PRIVATE page:
www.smart-persuasion.com/pain-of-paying

Principle 42

Sunk Cost Effect

(Kahneman & Tversky, 1970; Arkes & Blumer, 1985)

Description of the Principle:

The Sunk Cost Effect describes how people will often persist with a project or plan in which they have previously invested time, money or effort, even if they no longer want to. This is because they are influenced by the money and time already expended, rather than accepting that their investment is irretrievable.

Why this Principle works:

Experiments conducted by Arkes and Blumer in 1985 revealed that people prefer to do something less enjoyable if its perceived financial "benefit" is greater, and commit to doing something they don't want to if they have already paid for it. Have you ever not wanted to attend a concert or film, either because something more enjoyable was happening, or because you felt particularly ill and just wanted to stay in bed? Were you tempted to go anyway because you didn't want to 'lose' the money you had spent? Even though the money was gone either way, forcing yourself to attend made you feel like you had gotten some value from it, when it is likely you would have been happier had you just accepted the loss and done what you wanted.

How to use this Principle:

Introducing reminders that show customers how close they are to checking out, and reminding them of the time they've already invested on your site, will enhance their awareness of the Sunk Cost and increase the likelihood of them completing the purchase.

Concrete Application Example:

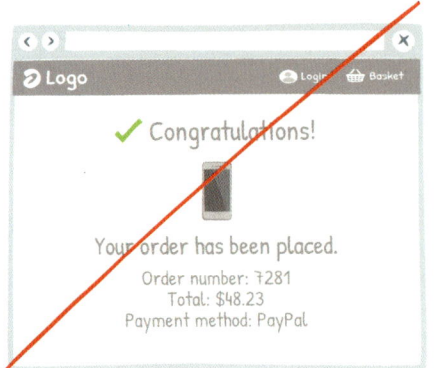 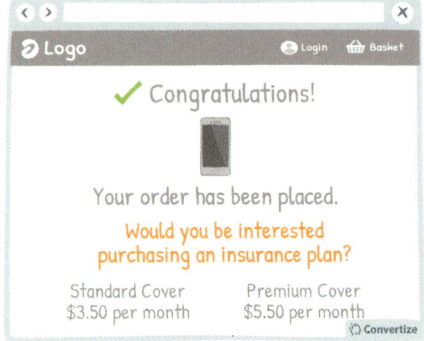

People will often continue with a project or plan for which they have already invested time or money, even if they no longer want to. The effect extends to situations where there is the potential for further losses. Showing your customers what they have invested so far is an effective way to reinforce their loyalty towards your products and convince them to make further commitments.

For example, offering protective cases or anti-virus software for electronic items would tap into the customer's fear that something might happen to their purchase and render their investment worthless.

If you are offering follow-up deals to a customer, you should remind them of the cost of their previous purchases. This provides a useful anchor but also leverages the Sunk Cost effect and increases the likelihood of them investing more in the future. Similarly, if you are offering additional features to an existing service, you should remind your customers of what they are already paying.

Sources and further examples:

Sources:
- Kahneman & Tversky, 1970
- Arkes & Blumer, 1985

Further examples on this PRIVATE page:
www.smart-persuasion.com/sunk-cost-effect

Principle 43

Reciprocity Principle

(Wedekind & Milinski, 2000; Cialdini, 2006)

Description of the Principle:

The Reciprocity Principle describes the human tendency to want to give something back after something has been received, whatever that might be. Sociologists believe that this psychological principle is part of the social norms that govern relationships. These norms create a feeling of obligation or indebtedness when someone does something for us. From a young age, we are socially "conditioned" to feel indebted to people who act in our favour.

Why this Principle works:

An example of this might be when someone buys you a Christmas gift simply because you gave them one: they feel compelled to do so based on the ingrained Reciprocity Principle. Conversely, the Reciprocity Principle can also work negatively, meaning that if someone wrongs you, you are likely to feel a compulsion to do the same to them, even if this would go against your usual character. In both cases, the principle is the same: you adjust your behaviour in relation to that of someone else's to maintain this "give-give" societal norm.

How to use this Principle:

The Reciprocity Principle has many sales tactic applications. For example, it is the root of the "rejection-then-retreat" sales technique. This technique consists of making a request that will probably never be accepted and then, once rejected, making a more reasonable request. Your customer will recognise that you have made a concession, and will feel obliged to reciprocate. In digital marketing, giving away something for free can hook a customer in and motivate them to want to give something back. Content marketing strategies that rely on giving customers useful and interesting information before asking them for anything in return also use this principle.

Concrete Application Example:

It is proven that we are more likely to give something to someone if they have given something to us already. The desire to reciprocate such behaviour is strong and can certainly lead to action and conversion. Giving your visitors information or knowledge for free will activate this desire to give something back. Your customers will be more inclined to buy, register or subscribe if you have previously provided them something they deemed useful. This needn't be anything too spectacular - simply letting them know that you are offering free delivery or a discount coupon will trigger this reciprocity bias.

Sources and further examples:

Sources:
- Wedekind & Milinski, 2000
- Cialdini, 2006

Further examples on this PRIVATE page:
www.smart-persuasion.com/reciprocity-principle

Fear of Missing Out (FOMO)

Principle 44

(Przybylski, Murayama, DeHaan & Gladwell, 2013)

Description of the Principle:

Fear of Missing Out is the anxiety caused by not taking part in a social occasion, new experience or other satisfying event. This fear of possible regret leads to a desire to stay continually connected with what others are doing, to feel that one is always in-the-know or "in touch". This psychological principle is most notably evident in the way in which certain people become addicted to social media and their mobile phones, constantly checking them in order to see what others are doing and to be sure they are not missing out on something.

Why this Principle works:

We fear that others are having more rewarding life experiences than us, and feel compelled to constantly check whether "the grass is greener". We also feel the need to stay informed about what other people are doing.

FOMO has several consequences for individuals' behaviour: it can lead some people to say "yes" to everything, whilst others avoid making decisions because they are worried something better will come along. In both cases, it can trigger negative emotions such as boredom, loneliness and frustration as it leads us to only see things in terms of "missed opportunities" rather than making the most of those things we do experience.

How to use this Principle:

In the commercial world, FOMO can certainly be a factor in motivating consumers to buy. Brands employ FOMO in advertising and marketing campaigns to make consumers feel as though they will be missing out if they don't own a particular product. Momentary marketing, for example, uses transient social media platforms to target FOMO with flash sales and ephemeral content that offers short-term deals, which prompts customers to remain "on the pulse" and to make quicker purchases.

Concrete Application Example:

Displaying the number of items left in stock will motivate people to make their purchase more quickly in order to avoid missing out.

The more difficult or urgent it is to acquire an item, or the more easily one could miss out, the more value that item is perceived to have. Visitors will then feel the urgency to buy it before it sells out.

Sources and further examples:

Sources:
- Przybylski, Murayama, DeHaan & Gladwell, 2013

Further examples on this PRIVATE page:
www.smart-persuasion.com/fear-of-missing-out-fomo

Illusion of Control

Principle 45

(Langer, 1975)

Description of the Principle:

The Illusion of Control, named by the Psychologist Ellen Langer in 1975, shows that humans have the tendency to believe that we can control or influence anything. Even regarding events that are totally random, we imagine ourselves to be capable of affecting the outcome. This Illusion of Control allows us to avoid the anxiety that can be induced by situations that are out of our control. For example, in a casino, you will often see a player blowing on the dice or throwing them with a certain force in an attempt to obtain the results they want from their roll.

Why this Principle works:

The throw of the dice cannot be influenced, as it is completely random, but these actions give the player the necessary Illusion of Control to feel comfortable in their situation. In 1975, psychologist Ellen Langer conducted an experiment where participants were given the opportunity to buy a lottery ticket for one dollar. The first group was given the option to choose their own lottery ticket, whereas the second group was simply given one at random. Participants were then asked whether they would consider selling on their lottery ticket and, if so, what price they would ask for it. The results showed that the first group, which had chosen their own tickets, were less willing to sell it on. If they were, they asked for a price that was at least four times more expensive than those from the second group were stating. This shows that the participants from the first group were affected by the Illusion of Control, believing their tickets to be of more value and more likely to win than those from the group who were given their tickets at random.

How to use this Principle:

The Illusion of Control has numerous applications in business and digital marketing. Giving your customers the impression that they are in control of any transactions will help to avoid the negative feelings attached to uncertainty. For example, customers will feel more positive if you allow them to select filters or options that enable them to control their searches. During the purchase process, it also helps to make it clear that they are able to make all decisions according to their own desires and wishes (by offering different payment methods, delivery options, etc.). The more you can give your customers control over certain elements of your site, the more you will incite their positive feeling of control and encourage conversions.

Concrete Application Example:

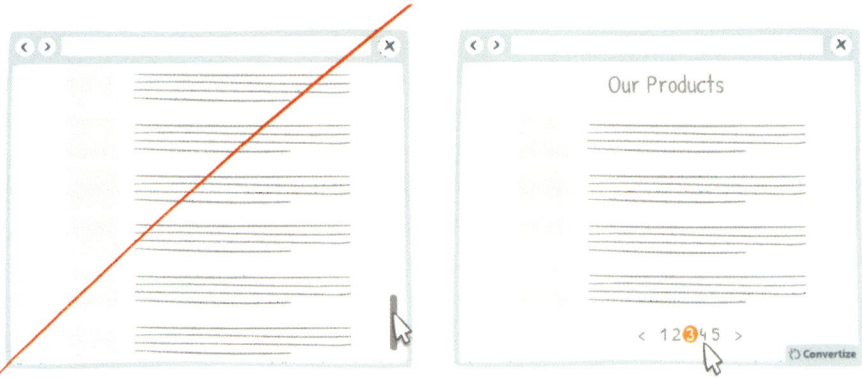

On eCommerce product pages, it is essential that you choose the right way to display your products to provide your customers with the most intuitive environment to start making choices. People tend to become overwhelmed by an excessive amount of choices.

With infinite scrolling, it can often seem as though the the product choice is never-ending, which can lead to frustration and a lack of focus. It is better to use either page numbers or a "load more" option. With page numbers, people can quickly see how many choices their search results have brought back and can decide whether to continue to add further filters. Using a "load more" function has the advantage of reducing a page's loading speed, whilst also giving customers access to another block of products at any time. These two functions give the customer more control over the products they are viewing, which will also immediately make them feel more positive towards your offers.

Sources and further examples:

Sources:
- Langer, 1975

Further examples on this PRIVATE page:
www.smart-persuasion.com/illusion-of-control

Attention & Perception

How to capture your visitors' attention and make your offers more persuasive

Von Restorff Effect

Principle 46

(Von Restorff, 1933; Taylor & Fiske, 1978; Gardner, 1983)

Description of the Principle:

The Von Restorff Effect (named after the psychiatrist who first studied it, Hedwig von Restorff) describes our tendency to remember things that stand out. In other words, we are more likely to remember the unusual. For example, in a list of words that are all written out identically (same size, colour, font, etc.) with one exception (one is in red, say), we will obviously notice this one and remember it more clearly. This principle can be applied to all manner of things: words, products, images, communications, or an unexpected event in an otherwise ordinary setting.

Why this Principle works:

This effect is due to the contrast evoked between one element and the others, which causes our brains to wake up and pay more attention. The result is that the incongruous element will not only be noticed, but will also stick in our brains for longer. Von Restorff showed in her studies how our eyes are constantly on the lookout for things that disrupt the norm, meaning we are constantly waiting to have our attention seized by anything out of the ordinary. This principle is also known as the Isolation, Prominence or Distinction Effect, as it is caused by the very fact of being presented with an element that is at odds with everything else.

How to use this Principle:

This principle is often used in the world of marketing and advertising to engage a target audience, and is particularly useful in this age of multiple communication platforms. An advert that stands out from the rest (be that through its tone, visuals or message) will be more effective.

Concrete Application Example:

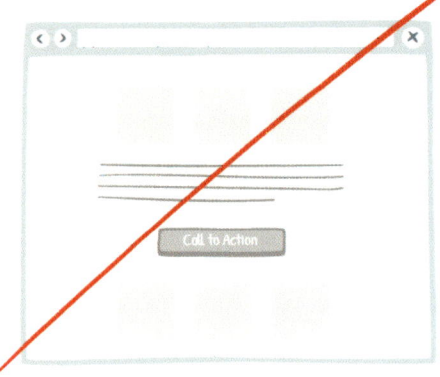 

The objective of a Call To Action (CTA) button is to encourage your visitors to do something in particular. Choosing a contrasting button colour and size will make it more prominent and salient on your page so that your visitors are more likely to click on it.

Sources and further examples:

Sources:
- Von Restorff, 1933;
- Taylor & Fiske, 1978
- Gardner, 1983

Further examples on this PRIVATE page:
www.smart-persuasion.com/von-restorff-effect

Gaze Cueing

Principle 47

(Perrett, Hietanen, Oram & Benson, 1992; Baron-Cohen, 1995; Emery, 2000; Frischen, Bayliss & Tipper, 2007)

Description of the Principle:

Gaze Cueing is the way in which we pay particular attention to the gaze and line of sight of others when looking at a face. We often find our own gaze being directed by someone else's.

Heatmap of a landing page with 2 different images

Why this Principle works:

Scientists have shown that the human gaze is an important social stimulus. From birth, we use our parents' gazes to learn about the world. In fact, eyes are a considerable source of information regarding the emotions, intentions and desires of other people. Studies have shown that 55% of information transmitted during a face-to-face conversation relies on visual contact. The eyes are a central factor in our social interactions and have an immense power over us, attracting our attention far more than other features or stimuli.

How to use this Principle:

There are numerous communication and marketing techniques that make use of Gaze Cueing. For example, websites often use the human face (photos, etc.) in their adverts or on their homepage and are careful to place important elements (such as Call To Action buttons, etc.) within the gaze path of the model. This helps to ensure that the website visitor has their gaze automatically drawn towards the desired elements of the page.

Concrete Application Example:

As humans, we have a natural tendency to follow others' gazes. It is an important social stimulus and often the way we learn about the world as we are growing up.

This can therefore be an effective way of drawing your website visitors' attention towards a particular element on your page. Not only that, but it also increases chances that they will convert: the presence of another human face gazing towards the desired action can increase a user's motivation to act.

Sources and further examples:

Sources:
- Perrett, Hietanen, Oram & Benson, 1992
- Baron-Cohen, 1995
- Emery, 2000
- Frischen, Bayliss & Tipper, 2007

Further examples on this PRIVATE page:
www.smart-persuasion.com/gaze-cueing

Visual Cueing

(Posner, 1980; Hommel, Pratt, Colzato & Godijn, 2001; Tipples, 2002)

Description of the Principle:

A visual cue is a signal that our brain focuses on out of everything that crosses our visual path. Only about 1% of what we see is constructed by our eyes, with the rest being formed by our brain. Our brain is particularly susceptible to Visual Cueing because it is impossible to notice and pay full attention to everything that passes in front of our eyes, and a visual cue gives some direction as to what to focus on. Everything we see (as well as hear, smell, etc.) is just a small portion of the "sensory landscape" that surrounds us at all times.

Why this Principle works:

There are many common visual cues that we have trained our brains to notice. Arrows are a very common visual cue, used for everything from lighting the way to an emergency exit to telling you in which order you should read infographics. They are synonymous with movement and progress, so are particularly effective both for directing attention and encouraging people to continue on a certain path.

How to use this Principle:

Visual Cueing is an important tool for use in any type of marketing and can be particularly effective online where our senses are overloaded with visual information. Making use of a visual cue such as an arrow will greatly increase the chances that a visitor's attention will be drawn towards a particular element.

They will then be more likely to follow through and engage with it (for example, by clicking on a CTA or filling out a form).

Concrete Application Example:

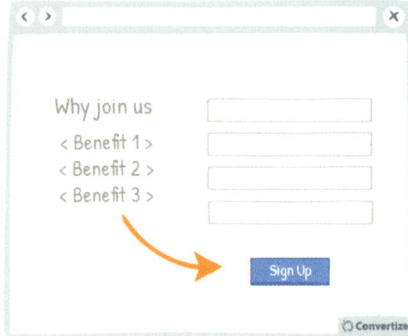

Your visitors' attention will be drawn towards familiar visual elements (like arrows) as they will notice and understand these visuals more quickly than any other information on the page.

Using this kind of visual stimulus is an effective way to draw immediate attention to your Call To Action (or anything else), increasing the chance that your visitors complete the desired action (clicking on the button).

Sources and further examples:

Sources:
- Posner, 1980
- Hommel, Pratt, Colzato & Godijn, 2001
- Tipples, 2002

Further examples on this PRIVATE page:
www.smart-persuasion.com/visual-cueing

Risk Compensation

(Peltzman, 1975)

Description of the Principle:

Risk Compensation, which was studied in detail in relation to motorway accidents by Dr. Sam Peltzman in 1975, describes the way that humans are more likely to take greater risks when they feel protected by certain factors.

Why this Principle works:

Peltzman found that measures taken to reduce road traffic accidents actually had no real effect at all. People felt like they were safe because they were required by law to wear their seatbelt or because their car was fitted with anti-lock brakes. However, this meant that they were actually more likely to drive faster or more dangerously close to the cars in front, believing themselves to be in a reduced state of risk.

How to use this Principle:

Understanding Risk Compensation is important for digital marketing. Making your customers feel that your website is a safe place to shop will encourage them to do so. If they feel secure and happy, they will be more likely to actually make purchases, and even spend more than they would have done otherwise. Adding "https" (protocol for secure communication), trust badges, and testimonials to your site will make your customers feel like they're shopping in a secure environment. This will give them the confidence to make purchases on your website.

Concrete Application Example:

If you use a special service phone number, your customers will be reluctant to call as they will expect high call charges and long wait times. This will make your business seem as though it is trying to extort money out of people, and it will lose credibility. Your potential customers will perhaps be more likely to search elsewhere than phone this number to find an answer they are looking for. Therefore, using a more recognisable, regular phone number will inspire more confidence and encourage people to call. It is also advisable to add your customer service opening hours so that potential customers have the chance to call you when it best suits them. This will have the knock-on effect of making your website seem transparent and unlikely to introduce unexpected costs in the course of purchasing something. Users will then be more prepared to make a purchase.

Sources and further examples:

Zero-Risk Bias

Principle 50

(Baron, Gowda & Kunreuther, 1993)

Description of the Principle:

Zero-Risk Bias is an irrational preference for options that eliminate risk, over those which only partly reduce a much larger risk. It leads us to undervalue some options, even when they have the potential to reduce the overall risk by a greater amount. So, when presented with two options, we will tend to choose the one that eliminates a small risk completely rather than the one that decreases a large risk by a greater amount.

This is because we have a cognitive bias that leads us to crave certain outcomes when we make decisions. Irrationally, we prefer to have a few guaranteed benefits rather than the possibility of much more significant benefits.

Why this Principle works:

For example, researchers analysed financial investment decisions made during the 2008 economic crisis and found they were heavily influenced by the Zero-Risk Bias. During this time of economic incertitude, investors were much more likely to lean towards "sure bets" such as governmental investments than towards private investments that may have seemed more risky - although would have had much bigger payouts had they come in. Therefore, most people were opting for a much smaller but more guaranteed return than higher-risk, higher-reward options.

Research has found that a large number of important political and economic decisions are influenced by Zero-Risk Bias. For example the implementation of laws removing any carcinogenic elements from food - regardless of the actual health risks or benefits - and the demand for the total decontamination of hazardous sites. These come from a focus on the complete elimination of risk in specific circumstances, rather than on the biggest possible reduction in risk.

How to use this Principle:

If you can attach a zero-risk quality to your products or services, then customers are more likely to make a purchase, selecting it over other options that may contain an element of risk. Remembering that people will most often choose the elimination of risk over a greater decrease (for example, when asked whether they would prefer the option that decreased risks from 5 to 0% or from 50 to 25%, people overwhelmingly chose the former despite the fact that the decrease in risk is nowhere near as significant) you could present your products as a solution to eliminate an issue completely.

Concrete Application Example:

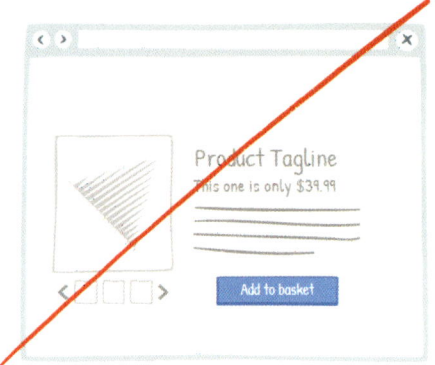 

You should prominently advertise a guarantee or refund policy. This will eliminate the risk associated with purchasing something, leveraging the customer's Zero-Risk Bias.

You could also use this to make more expensive products comparatively more attractive to customers. For example, let's say you offer two similar products, one that is better value for money but doesn't have a great returns policy, and another that is much more expensive but offers a 30-day money back guarantee.

Customers are more likely to opt for the more expensive option because they feel as though there is no purchasing risk attached.

Sources and further examples:

Sources:
- Baron, Gowda & Kunreuther, 1993

Further examples on this PRIVATE page:
www.smart-persuasion.com/zero-risk-bias

Principle 51

Attention Ratio

(Schwartz, 2004, Kahneman, 2011)

Description of the Principle:

The Attention Ratio principle is based on the fact that people are more likely to follow through on an action if their focus is concentrated and their attention is not split between lots of different elements. This is because having too much choice, information or visual stimuli overwhelms the human brain resulting in indecision and distraction. This is especially applicable to the internet where we are bombarded with information, links and contrasting visuals all the time. As many of us know, this can make it difficult to focus, follow through on our intended course of action or complete even simple tasks! The principle of Attention Ratio suggests that the value of interactive features on a web page is reduced in proportion with the total number of features displayed. The number of links you provide should be limited to the conversion goals you have (which, ideally, should be only one).

Why this Principle works:

If you are trying to convince your customers to buy a certain product or service, you should have a landing page that highlights just that one thing and leaves them a clear path towards the purchasing goal. If you surround that product with lots of other deals or information – such as events, sales coming up, or invitations to sign up for newsletters or other unrelated deals – your customer will become distracted and is unlikely to complete the purchase.

Imagine, for example, that you received an invitation for a gallery opening in the post and you decide to go. However, on the way, you notice that the gallery has put up signs outside the entrance with suggestions about other places you might like to visit. There are places to eat and local sites that you might be interested in. The chances are, you will be distracted by these. You may decide that you are hungry or that you would like to see that famous church. In the end, you may not even make it to the gallery...

How to use this Principle:

The same applies for digital marketing – don't distract your customers from your main goal. If you send out a newsletter for a specific campaign, say a half-price sale on your latest publication, then the link provided should lead to a landing page (never just your homepage), and that landing page should only have information about the publication on sale. There should be only one Call To Action button that leads the customer straight to the purchase of the sale item. By focusing your customer's attention rather than dividing it, your conversion rate should increase dramatically.

Concrete Application Example:

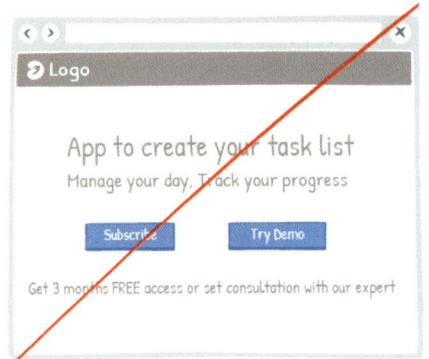
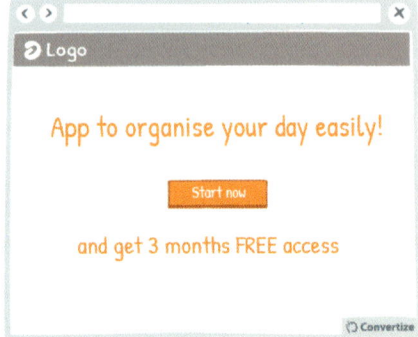

People respond best to clear, direct information, and are easily distracted by unnecessary demands on their attention. To avoid this, follow the simple yet effective 1-1-1 rule on your landing pages: 1 value proposition, 1 clear message, 1 Call To Action. Any additional information could distract your customers from your main goal and Call To Action, whereas using the 1-1-1 rule will focus customer attention and could therefore increase conversions.

Sources and further examples:

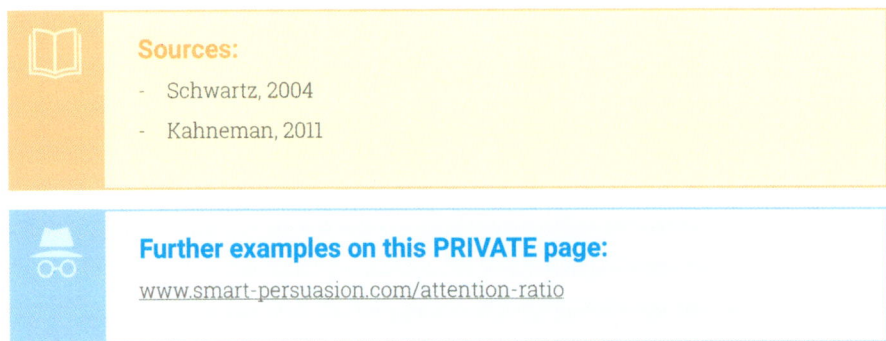

Aesthetic-Usability Effect

Principle 52

(Bloch, 1983; Norman, 2002)

Description of the Principle:

The Aesthetic-Usability Effect, studied by Donald A. Norman (2002), states that the more aesthetically pleasing a product is, the more usable it is perceived to be and the more likely it is to be used regardless of functionality. The reason for this Aesthetic-Usability Effect is that when a product or service is aesthetically pleasing to a consumer, they build an emotional relationship with it. This relationship breeds a sense of loyalty, and the consumer will stick by their choice even if they encounter problems with it. According to Bloch (1983), "visual appearance is the first thing a potential buyer notices about a product". Customers are more sympathetic to faults or failures if a design is aesthetically pleasing, leading them to believe that the better-looking option is the better option overall.

Why this Principle works:

For example, numerous studies have found that, technically, Apple products are not as usable as others on the market - meaning, people get tripped up more frequently and have a harder time understanding how to use the product than with other similar devices. However, Apple users either don't notice or don't care because Apple products are so aesthetically pleasing. The same concept has been found to be true of Mini Cooper cars, which have a lot of quirks (like the speedometer being located where the radio should be and the clock found on the ceiling). People forgive these minor anomalies simply because they like the way it looks.

How to use this Principle:

This principle has numerous applications in web design: when a customer visits a website, they are likely to prefer those they enjoy looking at and feel good about using, even if they don't perform the tasks as effectively as another. It is therefore important to foster a positive attitude to your website by using an aesthetically appealing design. If you can encourage positive feelings such as loyalty and affection, you will attract long-term users and ultimately be more successful.

Concrete Application Example:

A mobile-friendly checkout page is essential to ensure that people follow through with their purchase. A checkout page that is mobile responsive will not only be more aesthetically pleasing, but will also be easier to use. Furthermore, the checkout page is arguably the most important on your website. If you ensure that the checkout process is simple, and the page itself is well-designed, your users will be motivated to complete their payment.

If they arrive at the checkout on their mobile and are unable to see all the necessary information, or if it is difficult for them to complete their payment, this could result in lost sales.

Sources and further examples:

Sources:
- Bloch, 1983
- Donald Norman, 2002

Further examples on this PRIVATE page:
www.smart-persuasion.com/esthetic-usability-effect

Principle 53

Contrast Principle

(Cialdini, 2007; Kahneman, 2011)

Description of the Principle:

The Contrast Principle, first studied by Robert Cialdini in his 2007 book The *Psychology of Persuasion*, explores the way in which our perceptions are formed by comparison. When we experience similar things in succession, we evaluate the second by comparing it with the first. We form an enhanced or diminished perception of the second thing, based on how it compares to the first.

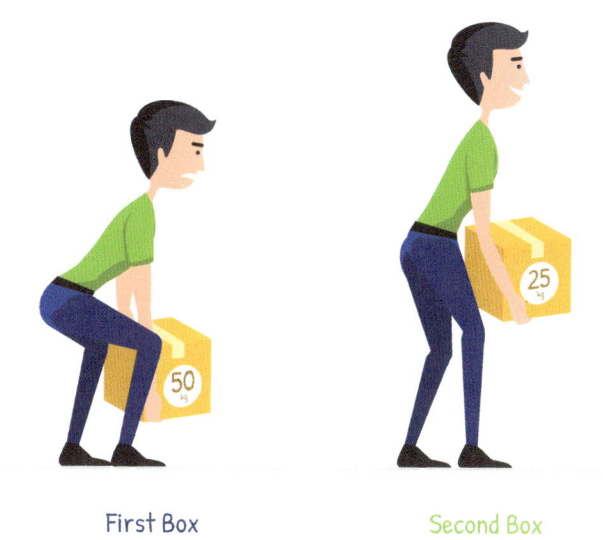

First Box · Second Box

For example, when you pick up a heavy box and then a lighter one, the second box will appear lighter than it really is.

Why this Principle works:

This Contrast Principle is due to the fact that our brain evaluates things based on the mode of comparison that is most easily accessible at that given moment, rather than the most suitable one. In other words, we tend to evaluate by comparative values, rather than by using more accurate, absolute values. Absolute values often aren't readily available for use, leading us to make biased judgments.

How to use this Principle:

The Contrast Principle is applied to all manner of judgments we might make on a day-to-day basis. For instance, let's say you're eating some strawberries and someone offers you a sugar-coated piece of candy. After tasting something extremely sweet, the strawberries will feel comparatively less sweet than they did before. In this way, the Contrast Principle can affect our judgments in relation to people, products, market values, and the values of many other attributes and characteristics.

The Contrast Principle has many applications in sales and marketing and is often used by brands to influence customers' perceptions of their products. For example, a technique often used by salesmen is to offer either a low quality or overpriced item alongside the one they really want you to buy. This influences your perception of the target product, making it seem like better value.

Concrete Application Example:

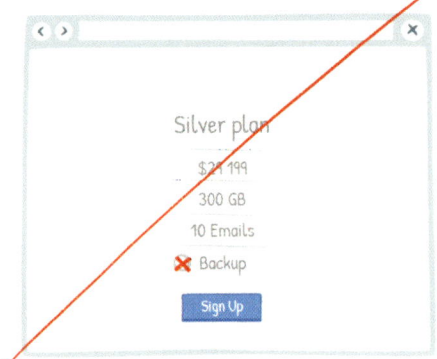
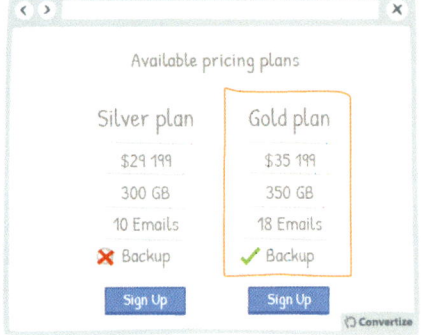

Providing a comparison table will allow your customers to immediately access all the information required for decision-making. Studies have shown that our perceptions are formed by using comparison techniques. When we experience similar things in succession or simultaneously, we evaluate the latter experience by comparing it to the first, as this is the easiest way to judge it.

A comparison table is therefore a useful means by which to encourage customers to opt for more expensive options that offer more features and benefits. Users evaluating your products will rarely select the lesser option when presented with the superior one as a direct alternative.

Sources and further examples:

Sources:
- Schwartz, 2004
- Cialdini, 2007
- Kahneman, 2011

Further examples on this PRIVATE page:

www.smart-persuasion.com/contrast-principle

Weber's Law

Principle 54

(Weber, 1834; Fechner, 1860)

Description of the Principle:

Weber's Law was originally postulated during research that Ernst Heinrich Weber carried out in 1834 to try and calculate the threshold for perceiving a change in weight. This was later applied to the general measurement of sensation and perception by Weber's student, Gustav Fechner. Weber's Law states that the threshold for perceiving change is dependent on the size or quantity of the original stimulus.

In other words, whether a change will be noticed is affected by how "big" the subject was beforehand. The more significant the change, in relation to this starting point, the more noticeable it is. Our sensorial capacity has limits, and there is an "absolute threshold" that describes the minimum amount by which stimulus intensity must be changed in order to be noticeable. Weber's Law shows that a difference of approximately 10 percent is the average point at which people are stirred to respond.

Why this Principle works:

Weber originally tested this using the sensation of weight, but it can be applied to a variety of sensory modalities (brightness, loudness, mass, length, etc.). It can also be applied to numerical values such as prices, the deletion of sections of text, or any other perceptions we might have. We can even take the well-known example of when a friend goes to the hairdresser without telling you: the likelihood of you noticing the new haircut will depend entirely on how different it is from beforehand. If it's just a trim without any changes to style or colour, then there's a strong likelihood that you won't even notice. However, if it is reduced from waist to shoulder-length, the change from the original will be so significant that it would be impossible to miss.

How to use this Principle:

Weber's law is often used in marketing, particularly with regards to price increases for products and services. It implies, for example, that it is possible to increase prices by small enough amounts – that fall under the "absolute threshold" – without your customers even noticing.

Concrete Application Example:

Avoid waiting until business needs necessitate a sharp increase in prices. Instead, anticipate and increase them gradually. Using frequent but small price increases will reduce the impact that these could have on your customers.

A sudden increase in price will immediately be more noticeable and will put many customers off, even if it is the first increase you have made in years (unless a significant improvement of the product justifies this increase). However, if you increase your prices regularly but by small increments, your customers will not have a concrete, long-standing reference price and therefore won't be as affected by these increases.

Sources and further examples:

Cognitive Dissonance

Principle 55

(Festinger, 1957)

Description of the Principle:

Cognitive Dissonance refers to a situation involving conflicting attitudes, beliefs or behaviours. Studied notably by Festinger (1957), this theory explains that when there is an inconsistency between attitudes, beliefs or behaviour, we are motivated to change something in order to eliminate this dissonance. The effect produces a feeling of discomfort that we automatically try to reduce by restoring the consistency. In other words, when we feel like our thoughts, feelings or actions are in conflict, Cognitive Dissonance sets in and gives us the feeling that something isn't quite right. Dissonance can be resolved in one of three basic ways: change of beliefs, change of actions or change of perception.

Why this Principle works:

For example, people who smoke are aware of the dangers smoking presents to their health. This creates a Cognitive Dissonance. In order to reduce this dissonance, they can either change their behaviour (by stopping smoking), change their beliefs (by finding stories about smokers who live to an old age), or change their perception (by telling themselves that it doesn't matter if smoking damages their health as "we've all got to die of something").

How to use this Principle:

Cognitive Dissonance has consequences for marketing strategies. For example, how well consumer satisfaction aligns with consumer expectation will affect how likely they are to be loyal to a product or service. When they don't align, it is called "post-purchase dissonance". It is therefore important to understand and effectively handle the expectations and grievances of both your current and future customers.

Concrete Application Example:

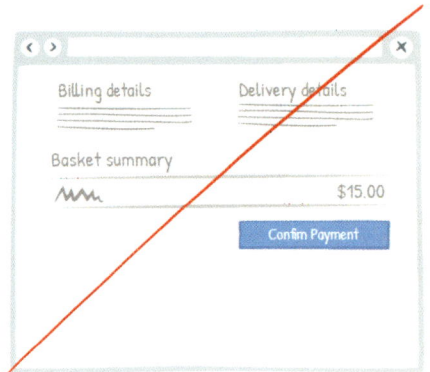 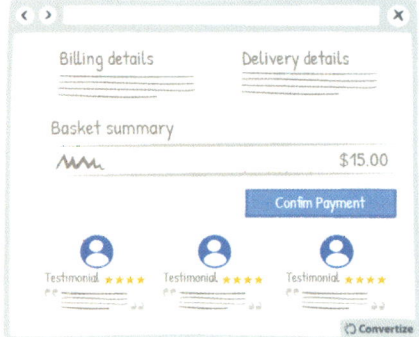

Post-purchase dissonance reduces customer satisfaction significantly more than minor faults or drawbacks. This might prevent someone from becoming a repeat customer, and could even lead to negative reviews.

By asking your customers why they bought a product, you ensure that their perception of it matches the reality. This will lead them to feel happier about their purchase when they receive it. Asking this question will also allow you to identify misleading product pages before they affect too many of your customers.

Sources and further examples:

Sources:
- Festinger, 1957

Further examples on this PRIVATE page:

www.smart-persuasion.com/cognitive-dissonance

Processing Efficacy

(Jacoby & Dallas, 1981)

Principle 56

Description of the Principle:

Processing Efficacy is based on the idea that objects differ in the fluency with which they can be processed. Since we engage more positively with things that we can process fluently, our judgement of something can be dramatically altered by how easy it is to understand. Fluent processing can be facilitated by several factors, such as repeated exposure, aesthetic attractiveness and even expressions that rhyme.

By contrast, low processing efficacy occurs when we find something difficult to interact with or understand. This requires more cognitive effort and strain, resulting in a negative feeling towards it.

Why this Principle works:

Several experiments have revealed that people are more likely to react positively to, and ultimately agree with, statements that are easier to read. The lack of cognitive strain involved in comprehending the statement improves the chances that it will be well-received. Simplicity is translated as beauty in the human mind, and we often judge something we perceive to be more beautiful as more positive and truthful.

How to use this Principle:

Processing Efficacy is an important consideration for digital marketers, especially with regards to content production or website design. A site's visual attractiveness, page load speed, and usability are all factors that will affect visitor satisfaction. Ultimately, this plays an important role in determining how persuasive your site will be.

Concrete Application Example:

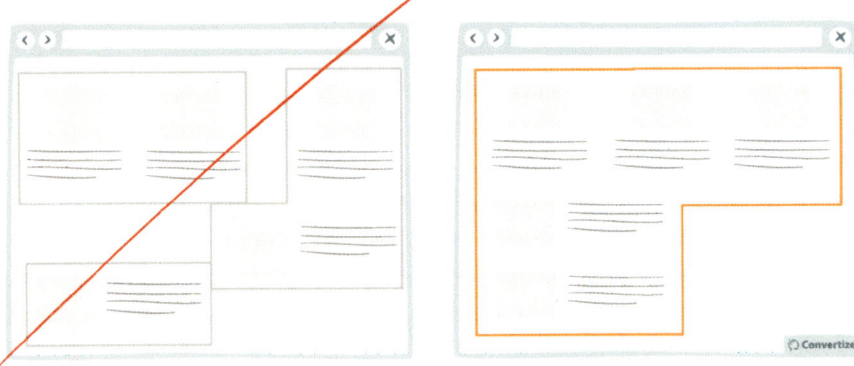

Make your blocks of content compact. You should avoid trapping negative (i.e. useless, empty) space within your layout. For example, in the left-hand image above, you can see that there are lots of empty spaces between the blocks of content. They serve no purpose and cause the layout to lack hierarchy and organisation which makes it more difficult to process. In the right-hand image the content is clearly laid out, making it easier to process and more appealing for the visitor to read. The easier and more pleasant you can make it for visitors to process your information, the more likely they are to stick on the page and convert. This is especially important as visitors will quickly abandon any page that doesn't immediately reveal its purpose.

Sources and further examples:

Sources:
- Jacoby & Dallas, 1981

Further examples on this PRIVATE page:
www.smart-persuasion.com/processing-efficacy

Endowment Effect

Principle 57

(Kahneman, Knetsch & Thaler, 1990)

Description of the Principle:

The Endowment Effect is the way in which people attribute a greater value to something when it is already in their possession. This is because we become psychologically attached and accustomed to owning things, causing our evaluation of them to change. They become more valuable in our eyes than things that we don't own. This explains why people will pay more to keep something they already own than they would to buy something new, and why many people find it difficult to throw things away.

Why this Principle works:

Kahneman, Knetsch & Thaler demonstrated the Endowment Effect with the following experiment. They divided students into three groups. Group A was given mugs, Group B chocolate bars, and Group C wasn't given anything but had to say whether they would have preferred a mug or a chocolate bar. Afterwards, Groups A and B were asked if they wanted to swap their respective "gifts". Whilst Group C didn't appear to have a particular preference for one or the other of these "gifts" (56% chose a mug, 44% a bar of chocolate), the other two groups were unwilling to exchange their items, having already attributed a value to them. Whilst Group C hadn't attached any real value to either item and would have been happy to have either, 89% of Group A wanted to keep their mug and 90% of Group B wanted to keep their chocolate bar. This clearly shows how once a human is in possession of an item (whether it be a mug, a chocolate bar, or something else entirely), a superior value is attributed to that thing than something that isn't in their possession.

How to use this Principle:

The Endowment Effect is utilised in certain sales and marketing techniques such as offering free trials. These are an effective way of allowing a customer to become accustomed to a product in the hope that, once their free trial has ended, they will have become attached to it. After experiencing owning the product, the customer will be reluctant to part with it. This should increase their perception of its value, and make them more willing to pay for it.

Concrete Application Example:

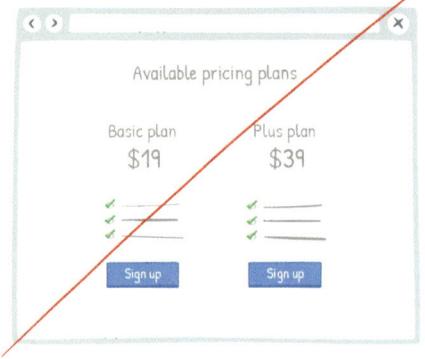 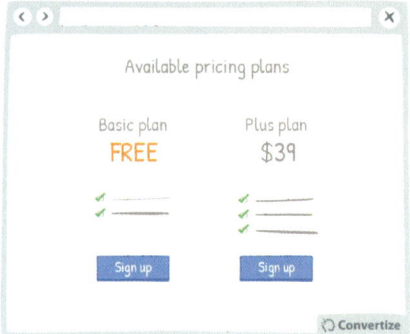

Offering customers a free trial, or creating a Freemium version of your product, is an easy way to take advantage of the Endowment Effect. By allowing someone to experience owning your product, you increase its value to them. When the time comes to make a decision, they will be more likely to purchase it.

The longer a free trial runs, the more powerful the endowment effect becomes. Alongside this, a customer faced with losing your product will experience Loss Aversion (Principle 5).

Freemium pricing restricts a customer's access to some of a product's features or limits the number of times they can use it. By balancing these restrictions carefully, you can expose customers to the Endowment Effect whilst maintaining the incentive to upgrade.

Sources and further examples:

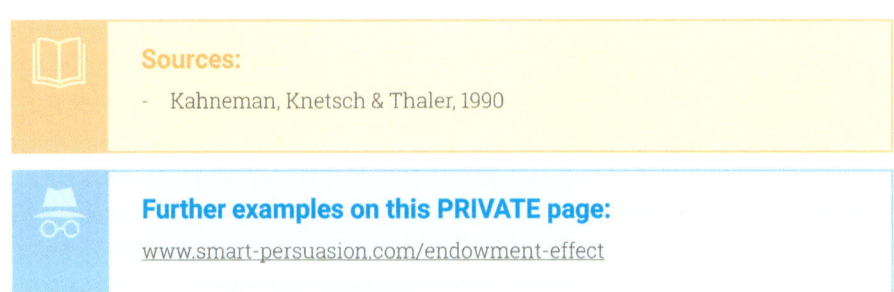

Split-Attention Effect

(Tarmizi & Sweller, 1988)

Principle 58

Description of the Principle:

The Split-Attention Effect occurs when sources of information that are mutually dependent for comprehension are separated, either spatially or temporally. For example, if you need both a diagram and written text to understand an instruction, but these are given to you on separate pages or at different times (Scenario A), you will find it much harder to digest and understand the information. By contrast, if both the text and the image were integrated into one visual (Scenario B), this would speed up the process of comprehension.

Why this Principle works:

The Split-Attention Effect is especially applicable to learning environments and techniques. Students who are given learning materials that combine all of the required information into one easy-to-read document will learn faster – and retain knowledge for longer - than those who have to take in the same information from multiple sources.

For example, let's say you are trying to assemble some flat-pack furniture. If the manufacturer has provided you with the diagrams on one piece of paper and written instructions on another, it would be difficult to follow. You would have to keep switching your attention between each corresponding piece of information. Integrating the diagrams and related text into one document would make comprehension much easier.

How to use this Principle:

Equally, if you're trying to sell something online and your customer requires multiple pieces of information to feel confident in their decision to purchase, this information needs to be presented clearly and in one location. This aids comprehension, means customers don't have to search for reassurance themselves, and avoids the risk of losing their attention and business.

Concrete Application Example:

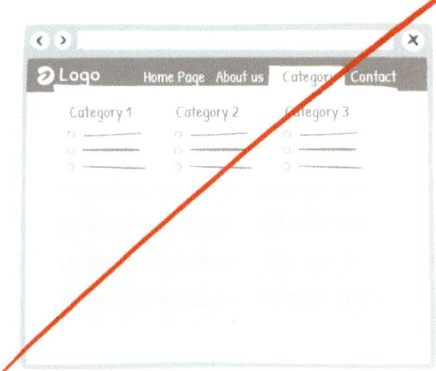 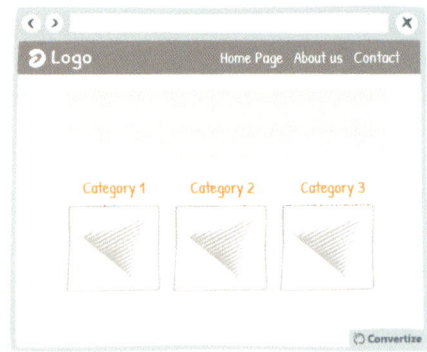

Because we interact with visual information in a different way to simple text, images are the most important element of your product page. Customers react more emotionally to visuals than to text and product images allow them to form a personal attachment to the object.

Giving potential customers the option to view multiple images of a product, perhaps from different angles, allows them to examine the item in the same way that they would if shopping in a store. Not only does this ensure that they have all the information they need to make a purchase, but it conveys a sense of ownership and triggers the Endowment Effect (Principle 57)

Sources and further examples:

Sources:
- Taylor & Fiske, 1978
- Gardner, 1983
- Tarmizi & Sweller, 1988

Further examples on this PRIVATE page:

www.smart-persuasion.com/split-attention-effect

Principle 59

Perceived Value Pricing

(Mazumdar, Raj & Sinha, 2005; Thomas, Simon & Kadiyali, 2007; Poundstone, 2010; Lee & Zhao, 2014)

Description of the Principle:

Perceived Value Pricing explains the phenomenon by which our perceptions of a price and its value aren't necessarily determined by actual market price or financial worth, but rather by the way in which the price is presented to us. This is because human psychology is victim to a Price-Value Bias. When we decide how much something is worth, we are easily influenced by unrelated elements.

There are very few products and services available that are priced according to a real calculation of their monetary value. Businesses will charge what people are willing to pay. People will be willing to pay whatever is consistent with the perceived value of the purchase. Of course, this value is highly subjective. It will depend on how something is presented, and how the customer chooses to perceive it. In sales, the perceived value of a product is often altered by the way the price is framed. For example, the price could be broken down to show how much it would cost per day over a year, which makes the amount seem much smaller. Suddenly, a $300 washing machine is re-evaluated as less than $1 per day over the course of a year – a bargain!

Similarly, the price can be reframed by simply changing the price tag from $100 to $99.99. The difference is minuscule but, in the psyche of the buyer, it becomes a much more attractive purchase. It's not just because the latter price is slightly cheaper; it's been proven that prices ending in '9' are more attractive to us – even when cheaper items may be on offer! In his book "*Priceless: The Hidden Psychology of Value*", William Poundstone explains how "we've been culturally conditioned to associate 9-ending prices with discounts and better deals."

Choosing the price you present has particularly important connotations when dealing with a large sum of money. Thomas, Simon, and Kadiyali (2007) analysed 27,000 real estate transactions and found that people paid more money for houses when the prices were very precise (i.e. were willing to pay $362,130 over $350,000). This has been explained by the fact that we associate the small numbers used in precise pricing (1, 2, 3, etc.) as having small values, and therefore when we see these numbers the value appears smaller than it is.

Why this Principle works:

The wording used to explain prices can also have an effect on the customer's perception of its value. Sometimes discounts can actually put off customers, as the terms "discount" and "bargain" can have negative connotations, making people believe the product is low quality. In order to counteract this, it is important to accompany the discount with a reason. As Mazumdar, Raj & Sinha (2005) noted, some large stores have found that giving a straight-forward reason for a discount or saving, such as a reduction in the cost price that has been passed on to the customer, helps to enhance the success of promotions.

How to use this Principle:

It's also important to remember that, in some cases, making a product appear more expensive actually helps sales because higher price tags already carry with them an intrinsic sense of value. If you're charging more money for something, people will naturally assume there is a reason for this and attach a higher value to that product. In marketing your product, it is important to know who your target audience is. This will help you to decide what type of Price-Value Bias will appeal to them most.

Concrete Application Example:

 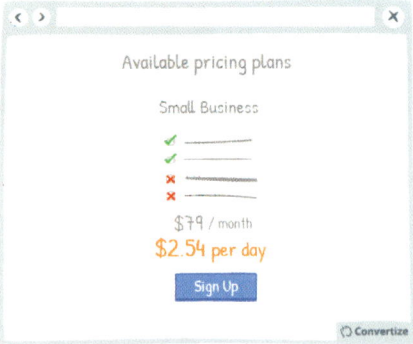

Rather than only showing the yearly or monthly cost of a subscription, it can be effective to also display the daily equivalent.

Studies have shown that we use a first piece of information as an anchoring point for any subsequent information we receive. Displaying the daily equivalent first or more prominently will lower your customers' perception of the cost. Displaying the daily equivalent of a monthly or yearly cost places emphasis on a smaller price which leads people to perceive it as cheaper or better value even though it is technically the same price.

It is also a simple yet effective way to lower people's perception of the cost. Displaying the daily equivalent of a monthly or yearly cost places emphasis on a smaller price which leads people to perceive it as cheaper or better value even though it is technically the same price.

Sources and further examples:

Sources:
- Mazumdar, Raj & Sinha, 2005
- Thomas, Simon & Kadiyali, 2007
- Poundstone, 2010
- Lee & Zhao, 2014

Further examples on this PRIVATE page:
www.smart-persuasion.com/perceived-value-pricing

Centre-Stage Effect

Principle 60

(Valenzuela & Raghubir, 2009;
Rodway, Schepman & Lambert, 2011)

Description of the Principle:

The Centre-Stage Effect is the way in which, when faced with a range of products presented side by side, we tend to be drawn towards the one situated in the middle. Valenzuela & Raghubir (2009) showed that people tend to assume that products placed in the centre (of a shop window, on a shelf, etc.) are the most popular. They assumed that these products were in a prominent position because they were a popular choice amongst other buyers. Central positioning acts as a social signal that biases us towards a particular product and makes it more likely that we will choose it. Research has shown that the Centre-Stage Effect is even more pronounced when we're buying something for someone else.

Rodway, Schepman and Lambert (2012) conducted a series of studies on this phenomenon and found that the Centre-Stage Effect comes into play when all the elements in a "line-up" are of a similar nature (whether that be in function or appearance). Whether the line-up is vertical or horizontal, or consists of real-life products or online images, seems to have no effect on the outcome.

During their research, they showed participants identical white socks lined up vertically in front of them, as well as a selection of images showing similar objects displayed horizontally on a webpage. In both cases, the majority of participants chose those that were in the middle.

How to use this Principle:

The Centre-Stage Effect has numerous applications in advertising, business and marketing. This bias suggests that, by positioning a product that we wish to attract attention to centrally (for example, placing a high-margin option in the middle of a menu), we can increase the chance that it will be noticed by customers. The same principle allows online marketplaces such as Amazon and eBay to charge higher rates for adverts shown in the centre of their displays.

Concrete Application Example:

 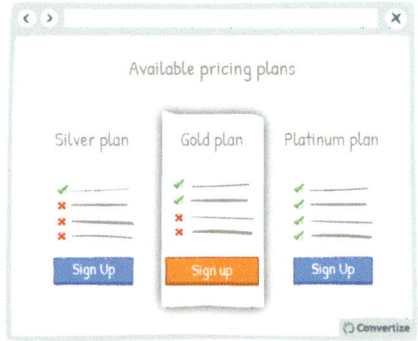

When you have a default pricing plan (the option you would prefer people to choose), you can make this option more attractive by designing it to stand out from the others.

Placing it in the middle and bringing it to the front (either by highlighting it or putting the Call To Action button in a different colour) will make it attract people's attention and make them more likely to choose it.

Furthermore, designating something as the default option makes people more likely to select it, as they assume it is most popular. For more on this, see the Default Effect (Principle 15).

Sources and further examples:

Sources:
- Valenzuela & Raghubir, 2009
- Rodway, Schepman & Lambert, 2011

Further examples on this PRIVATE page:
www.smart-persuasion.com/centre-stage-effect

Salience Effect

Principle 61

(Guido, 2001; Spool, 2002; Harwood, Raman & Hewstone, 2006)

Description of the Principle:

The Salience Effect describes the way in which individuals are drawn to certain features and retain particular information. Our brains struggle to give equal attention to multiple things at once and therefore register them according to a subconscious hierarchy. The salient elements are those which are given priority.

The Salience Effect can come into play for multiple reasons. It could be that a particular element is noticeably distinguishable from its surroundings (for example, a sudden noise in a quiet environment or something that is lit up at night) and therefore attracts attention. Other elements may become salient over time as we gain the habit of noticing them only at a particular moment. For example, we may pay no attention to the cars passing us by in the street until the very moment we wish to cross over. Then these cars suddenly become our primary focus. Equally, what we do and our personal interests will affect what we find salient. Someone who works in fashion, for example, will be more likely to notice fashion-related details than someone whose primary interest is, say, music.

How to use this Principle:

The objective of marketing is to enhance the salience of a product, brand, or message. Using contrast is one way to do this. For example, consumers are so desensitised to the classic format of TV advertising that successful new ads have to break the mould to stand out.

Salience also depends on choosing the right moment. For example, if your customer is looking for a refrigerator, then the elements of your site that lead them towards information and offers on fridges will be immediately more salient to them than other unrelated links or offers. Equally, consumers will be more receptive to new elements once their primary reason for visiting your site has been taken care of. Jared Spool conducted research in 2002 studying user behaviour on a distribution website. He discovered that consumers are less likely to pay attention to elements that don't concern them before their primary purpose has been accomplished. Once a consumer's primary aim is achieved, other offers and products will become more salient.

Concrete Application Example:

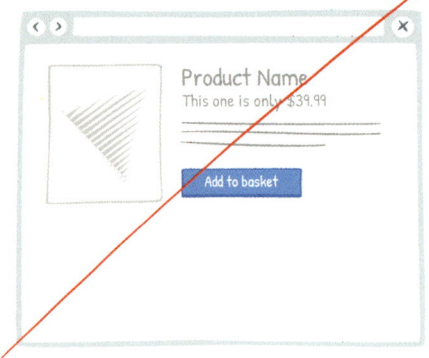 

Cross-selling is an effective way of increasing sales by proposing related products to your customers when they are in the process of viewing or purchasing something. These might be accessories (such as anti-virus software, for someone who is buying a computer) or otherwise related products (such as books by the same author).

People are always looking for guidance and will often follow the example of their peers when unsure about a choice. Introducing these cross-sells with "customers who bought this product also bought" or "people who viewed this item also looked at," can have a strong influence on the likelihood of your customers following these recommended items.

The fact that the products you're suggesting seem tailored to the customer and their needs will also increase engagement. Indeed, studies have shown that after making the initial decision to purchase we are more inclined to then buy additional items. This is based on a desire to justify our initial decision and remain consistent with it as per Commitment and Consistency (Principle 36).

Sources and further examples:

Sources:
- Guido, 2001
- Spool, 2002
- Harwood, Raman & Hewstone, 2006

Further examples on this PRIVATE page:
www.smart-persuasion.com/salience-effect

Representativeness Heuristic

Principle 62

(Kahneman & Tversky, 1972)

Description of the Principle:

The Representativeness Heuristic is a cognitive bias explored by Kahneman and Tversky in their article "Subjective Probability: A Judgment of Representativeness" (1972). It describes the way in which people misjudge the probability or frequency of an event by basing their judgement on superficial similarities rather than statistical calculations. The Representativeness Heuristic also explains the way in which we place objects in to a certain category simply based on a limited number of similarities. Even if something doesn't fit exactly into a known category, we will judge it to be the same if we can draw enough parallels. This shortcut leads us to judge the probability of something, or the category it fits into, based on intuition rather than objective or statistical reasoning.

Why this Principle works:

To give an example, if an individual sees three blackbirds fly past in succession, they might expect the fourth bird to go past to be black too, and even assume that maybe there are only black birds in that particular area. These would be biased assumptions based on a mental shortcut that relies on generalisation rather than statistical probability. Mathematically speaking, without knowing any statistics related to the ornithological distribution in the area, the fourth bird is just as likely to be any other colour as it is to be black.

How to use this Principle:

The Representativeness Heuristic affects digital marketing in several ways. In order to make your product appear as attractive as possible to your customers, you can highlight the similarities of this product to another that you know your customer likes (perhaps something they've previously bought). You can also make use of this principle to ensure that the products and services you are offering match up with their expectations based on representative models.

Furthermore, you can make your website easier to navigate by using recognisable icons to represent sections. For example, in the checkout process, use small icons in a bar at the top to show users each stage of the process and which position they are at. This will make it simpler to follow, and encourage users to complete it.

Concrete Application Example:

Your Call To Action (CTA) is a button - you need it to look like one! Adding depth to your CTA by using a border, bevel or shadowing will help to clearly distinguish it as a button that is there to be clicked on.

A visual effect to indicate that it is clickable will make it much easier for people to see automatically which parts of the page are interactive and will lead them to engage without any frustration. Ultimately this improved user experience should lead to more conversions.

Sources and further examples:

Sources:
- Deci, 1971
- Kahneman & Tversky, 1972
- Ryan, 2008

Further examples on this PRIVATE page:
www.smart-persuasion.com/representativeness-heuristic

Principle 63

Picture Superiority Effect

(Paivio, 1971; Hockey, 2008)

Description of the Principle:

The Picture Superiority Effect relates to the fact that the human brain learns and retains information much better when it comes in the form of images rather than words. Therefore, visual sources can have a much greater and more lasting impact than text. Allan Paivio (1971) explains this principle with the theory of "dual coding". We retain images better than words because they are coded twice in our memory. Paivio explains that our memories take in information using two different codes: "verbal" codes and "image" codes. When we're presented with an image it generates both a verbal and an image code (taking the visual image and generating a verbal code using an associated word or phrase), whereas when we're presented with something that is solely verbal, it only generates the one verbal code. When our brain then wants to retrieve information, it finds it easier to locate the images because they have been "dual coded". This is why we find it both easier to memorise and then later remember information that is presented in a visual manner.

Why this Principle works:

Hockey carried out an experiment in 2008 to demonstrate the Picture Superiority Effect. He asked participants to memorise both random pairs of words and random pairs of images. He then rearranged the pairs so that some of them were no longer with their original partners and asked the participants to identify those that had been changed. The results showed that people were able to identify the original image pairings more easily than the word pairings.

How to use this Principle:

Picture Superiority Effect can be utilised in many ways. Images are a useful aid for learning environments, helping people to learn and retain information more easily. They can also be used to increase engagement and message retention in marketing and advertising campaigns.

Concrete Application Example:

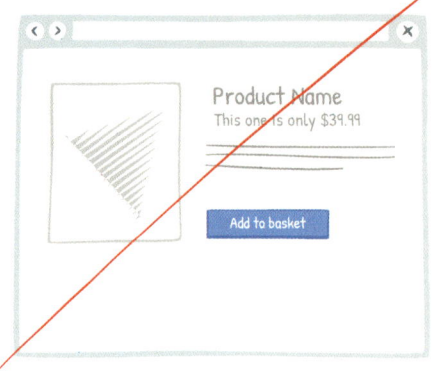 

Because we interact with visual information in a different way to simple text, images are the most important element of your product page. Customers react more emotionally to visuals than to text and product images allow them to form a personal attachment to the object.

Giving potential customers the option to view multiple images of a product, perhaps from different angles, allows them to examine the item in the same way that they would if shopping in a store. Not only does this ensure that they have all the information they need to make a purchase, but it conveys a sense of ownership and triggers the Endowment Effect (Principle 57).

Sources and further examples:

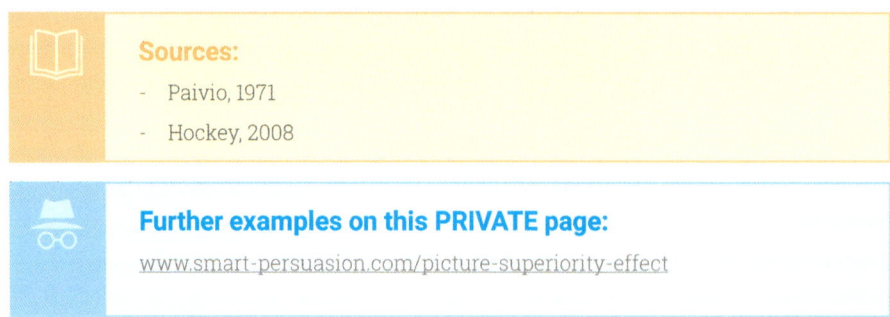

Sources:
- Paivio, 1971
- Hockey, 2008

Further examples on this PRIVATE page:
www.smart-persuasion.com/picture-superiority-effect

Principle 64

Visual Depiction Effect

(Elder & Krishna, 2012)

Description of the Principle:

The Visual Depiction Effect, notably studied by Elder & Krishna in 2012, describes how people are more inclined to buy a product when it is shown in a way which helps them to visualise themselves using it. Simply ensuring that your product is orientated in such a way that it could easily be picked up or used by a right-handed person (as the majority of people are) can vastly increase the interest a potential customer will show in this product. Similarly, it can also be effective to display a product being used by someone, without its packaging, or in the context we might use it in (such as showing a dinner set arranged on a table).

Why this Principle works:

Advertising a product using these tactics makes it easier for a customer to connect with the product and imagine it as part of their lives. The Visual Depiction Effect is particularly important for online marketing, where imagery plays an essential role as customers are unable to actually see the physical product.

How to use this Principle:

This principle is useful when you are trying to market products that people interact with. It's why websites selling clothing and footwear have multiple images of models wearing their products, as people can easily visualise how they look when worn.

Similarly, accessories such as fitness devices should be depicted actually being worn by someone. Not only does this help someone imagine themselves using the product, but it also gives customers a better idea of the scale of the product. Even software, which obviously isn't something you can easily show someone using, can be marketed using the Visual Depiction Effect. You could display a slideshow of screenshots on the screen of a laptop or create short demo videos of someone's screen as they use the software.

Concrete Application Example:

If your customer can visualise themselves using your product then they'll feel more inclined to buy it.

You can increase the chances of this happening by arranging product images so that your customers can imagine themselves with the product (for example, by showing what it looks like in someone's hand or picturing it being used).

These techniques will all help your customer to automatically connect and interact psychologically with the product, increasing the likelihood of them actually buying it.

Sources and further examples:

Sources:
- Elder & Krishna, 2012

Further examples on this PRIVATE page:
www.smart-persuasion.com/visual-depiction-effect

Principle 65

Physical Attractiveness

(Caballero & Pride, 1984; Kahle & Homer, 1985;
Kamins, 1990; Bower, 2001; Tsai & Chang, 2007; Buunk & Dijkstra, 2011)

Description of the Principle:

The principle of Physical Attractiveness explores the way in which we react to models used in advertising (whether that be online, in magazines or on TV).. Many researchers have studied this subject and found that, when used in an appropriate context, attractive models have a positive effect on an advert's effectiveness. If we find the model physically attractive, it improves a product's credibility (Kamins, 1990), enhances our desire to buy it (Kahle & Homer, 1985), and increases the attention we give to the advert (Caballero & Pride, 1984).

Why this Principle works:

Many hypotheses have been put forward to explain this phenomenon. The main one is a tendency to project the model's qualities (such as beauty or confidence) onto the product they're using. We imagine that owning the product will give us the same qualities.

However, this tendency to compare ourselves with the people we see in adverts can have unexpected effects. In other studies, notably by Bower in 2001, it has been shown that attractive models can diminish an advert's effectiveness. Customers compare themselves unfavourably to the model and associate their negative feelings with the product.

A model's physical appearance will influence us in some way, as we make subconscious judgements about them and the product. These could be positive, leading us to associate the product with luxury and success, or negative, creating feelings of distrust and jealousy. Caballero and Pride (1984) showed that using an attractive model to try and sell tissues was inneffective. It diminished the credibility of the advert, because someone who was unwell would not appear so attractive, damaging trust in the product.

How to use this Principle:

It is important to use Physical Attractiveness carefully when marketing a product. Using an attractive model can improve the desirability of your product, and increase the attention given to your marketing materials. However, when used inappropriately, it can also have a negative effect on your customers and the trust they place in your brand.

Concrete Application Example:

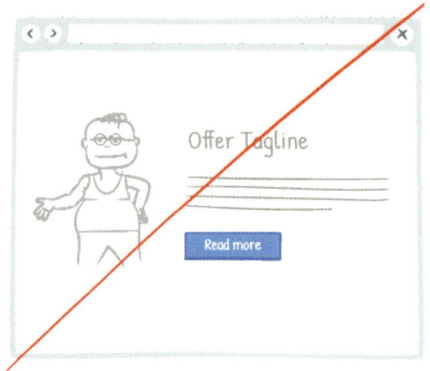 

Studies have shown that using a model to market a product increases its credibility, how much attention people pay to it, and how likely they are to want to purchase it. Your customers will project the positive qualities the model embodies (attractiveness, happiness, health) onto the product or service you are marketing and will want to buy it in order to also benefit from these.

What's more, by displaying one positive trait (the attractiveness of the model) to your customer, they are likely to project other positive traits onto your product, too. We have a tendency to use select information to make broader judgments. One positive attribute can lead us to assume that all the other attributes associated with something will be equally positive. For more on this, see the Focusing Effect (Principle 13).

It is worth noting that using attractive models isn't always appropriate, depending on what the product or service is that you offer on your site. It could harm credibility and reduce sales (if your customers are looking for medical products or a funeral service, for example).

Sources and further examples:

Sources:
- Kamins, 1990
- Bower, 2001
- Tsai & Chang, 2007
- Buunk & Dijkstra, 2011

Further examples on this PRIVATE page:

www.smart-persuasion.com/physical-attractiveness

Halo Effect

Principle 66

(Thorndike, 1920; Asch, 1946; Clifford, 1975)

Description of the Principle:

The Halo Effect is a cognitive bias in which people base their judgments about something on a small amount of unrelated information. For example, we tend to allow first impressions to inform our overall opinion of a new person.

Once we begin to like someone, due to a single agreeable trait, we arbitrarily award them other positive characteristics. Just one observation is enough to bias our entire image of a person.

Why this Principle works:

This cognitive bias was theorised by Thorndike in 1920 and later proven by Asch (1946) and Clifford (1975). Clifford demonstrated how people considered to be more attractive were often also deemed to be more intelligent as well, despite the two factors having no correlation. During his experiment, teachers were shown photos of unknown pupils and asked to make assumptions on several different elements of their characters (such as their intelligence or the likelihood of them achieving academic success).

The results showed that when given photos of more "attractive" pupils, the teachers described them as more likely to be intelligent or successful than others. There was no basis for these presumptions other than the fact that the one "positive" characteristic they had to go on (in this case, the attractive physical appearance) led them to subconsciously attribute other positive characteristics to these pupils.

However, the Halo Effect also works inversely. The "Devil Effect" shows how we are also likely to judge people negatively based on one single negative attribute. For example, we may demonstrate a negative sentiment towards someone that we don't even know simply due to the fact that they hang out with a crowd of people we don't like. Conversely, we may form a negative opinion of a whole group of people simply because one person we don't like is included in it.

How to use this Principle:

The Halo Effect has huge significance for brands and businesses. For example, a brand that is well-known for having one particular quality product will find that all of its other products are also assumed to be of a similar quality, even if this theory hasn't been tested. Similarly, when promoting a certain item or service, any good publicity generated will be attributed to the brand as a whole. This can lead to a much wider, more positive impact than any individual advertising campaign merits. In this way, certain marketing strategies use just one or two particular positive elements (such as a client testimonial or a popular celebrity endorsement) to cast an overall positive light on their brand image.

Concrete Application Example:

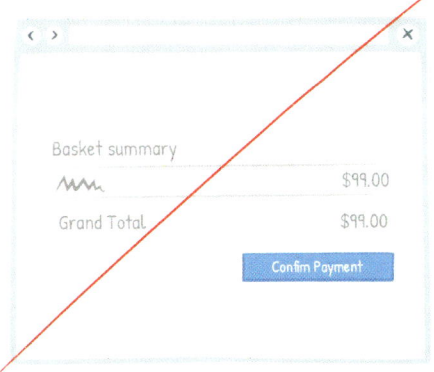 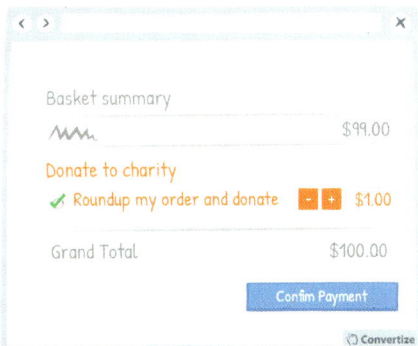

A single association can change the way people perceive your company or your brand. One way to take advantage of this is to showcase your relationship with a cause or charity that your customers care about.

By offering someone the chance to make a donation through your store, you acquire positive associations from the charity. For example, prompting customers to round up their basket total and donate the change to a local charity will make your store appear caring and trustworthy.

Sources and further examples:

Principle 67

Base Rate Fallacy

(Kahneman, 2011)

Description of the Principle:

Base Rate Fallacy, also known as base rate neglect, is an error which occurs when prior base rates are neglected when evaluating new information. In other words; it is the mind's tendency to ignore statistical context.

Why this Principle works:

The Base Rate Fallacy occurs when we are too quick to make judgments, ignoring base rates or probabilities in favour of new information. There is a famous "cab driver problem", illustrated by the behavioural psychologist Daniel Kahneman, which demonstrates this phenomenon clearly.

In his experiment, the subjects were presented with a fictional situation. They were told there had been a hit and run accident at night involving a taxi cab, and that the only eyewitness had identified the cab as being blue. They were told that there were two taxi companies in the city, one with green cabs (responsible for 85% of the cabs in the city), and the other with blue cabs (responsible for the remaining 15%). Finally, they were told that the court had tested the reliability of the eyewitness. In night-time conditions, the witness identified colours correctly 80% of the time.

Kahneman's subjects were then asked: "What is the likelihood that the cab involved in the accident was blue rather than green?" Most of the subjects said that that there was an 80% chance that the cab was blue.

This is an example of Base Rate Fallacy because the subjects neglected the initial base rate presented in the problem (85% of the cabs are green and 15% are blue). The problem should have been solved using Bayes' rule as follows:

- There is a 12% chance (15% x 80%) the witness correctly identified blue.
- There is a 17% chance (85% x 20%) the witness incorrectly identified green as blue.
- There is a 29% chance (12% + 17%) the witness will identify the cab as blue.
- This results in a 41% chance (12% ÷ 29%) the identification is correct.

How to use this Principle:

Base Rate Neglect is our tendency to misjudge the likelihood of a situation by not considering the statistics presented, but rather by focusing more heavily on the last piece of information available. This is particularly significant when presenting potential customers with information about reviews and testimonials Whilst the most important information to consider is the average customer satisfaction rating, visitors may be disproportionately persuaded by individual reviews (particularly if they are more recent or more emotive.) It is important to make sure that your customers see both the base rate of customer satisfaction and more recent individual reviews.

Concrete Application Example:

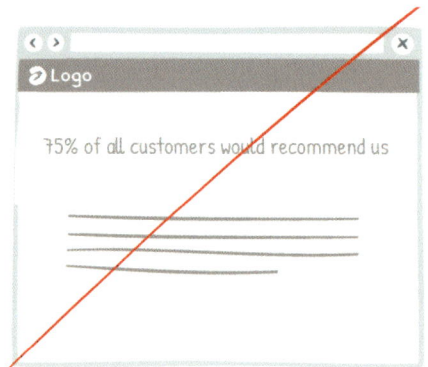
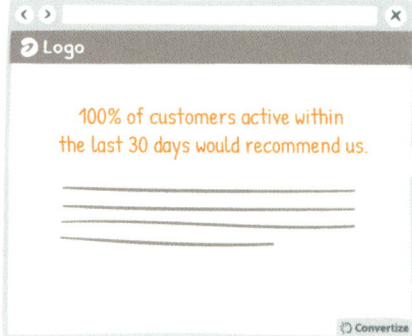

Most people overlook broad trends and focus on more recent or more specific information. This makes it difficult for companies and brands to leverage past success when appealing to new customers. The material you use for advertising or content marketing should be specific, up-to-date and relevant to the potential customer. This will make your communications more emotionally engaging.

Sources and further examples:

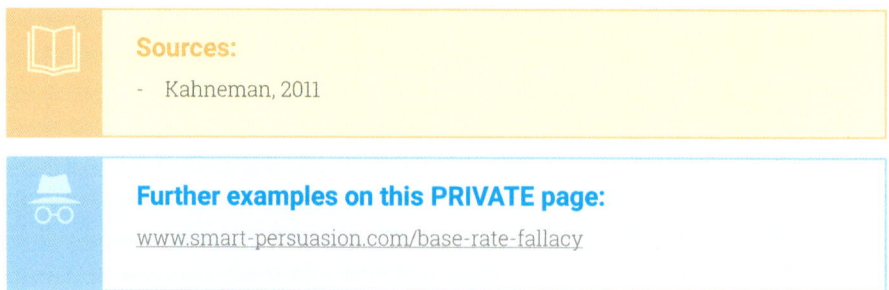

Social Biases

How social biases affect your customers, and what you can do with them

Principle 68

In-Group Bias

(Sumner, 1906; Tajfel, 1982; Maass & Arcuri, 1996)

Description of the Principle:

In 1906, sociologist William Sumner posited that humans are intrinsically more comfortable being within social groups, and that we are also inclined to believe our own group is superior to others. We tend to favour and place more merit on the opinions and actions of people from our own in-group, and we build up our social identity and self-esteem through belonging. People from our group remind us of this belonging, and are automatically given preferential treatment.

Why this Principle works:

Henri Tajfel (1982) conducted an experiment by splitting a class of 14-year old boys into arbitrary groups and then assigning them random tasks. These tasks eventually become competitive and money was assigned to winners. Despite the fact that they all knew each other and had alternative friendship groups outside of this experiment, Tajfel observed how quickly the boys formed strong allegiances to their assigned groups. They also began to make choices that would be to the detriment of the other groups.

For example, one of their last tasks was a hypothetical situation concerning the profit that could be made through selling art. The boys were given choices about which actions they could take. Some actions led to them making a profit, some led to all groups making a profit, and the final actions would lead to them making a profit whilst the other groups suffered a loss. Overwhelmingly the boys chose the latter option, seeking both to succeed and to cause other groups to fail.

How to use this Principle:

In the commercial world, the In-Group Bias is obvious in extreme brand loyalty. For example, people are proud of being an Apple user, and feel they have more in common with other people who also use Apple products. This creates a shared loyalty, and also a disconnection from those who are "outside" the group. On a smaller scale, the In-Group Bias is an effective way of gaining loyalty for your brand, and can be leveraged through membership schemes or by showing customer testimonials on your website.

Concrete Application Example:

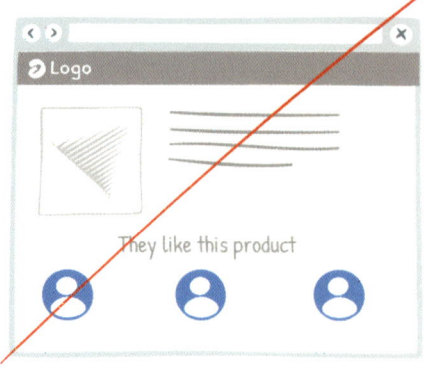
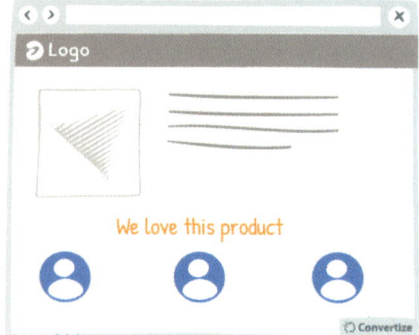

The power of "we" or "our" is not to be underestimated. We are social beings, and we feel most comfortable and positive when we are included as part of a group. Therefore, instead of excluding your visitor by using "they" or other third person pronouns, include them in the most basic way by using first person plural pronouns instead.

As demonstrated in the above example, first person pronouns can encourage your visitors to identify with previous customers. As a result, they will be influenced more strongly by the positive reviews. Using first person plural pronouns will make visitors feel as though they are already part of the group using the product or service, and are therefore more likely to follow through on any subsequent actions required to make this a reality.

Sources and further examples:

Sources:
- Sumner, 1906
- Tajfel, 1982
- Maass & Arcuri, 1996

Further examples on this PRIVATE page:
www.smart-persuasion.com/in-group-bias

Principle 69

Social Proof

(Sherif, 1935; Asch, 1956)

Description of the Principle:

This principle was first explored by social psychologist Sherif in 1935, and later developed by Asch in 1956. Social Proof is the idea that we are intrinsically driven to conform and so will often be influenced to copy others' decisions and actions, especially when we are hesitating or feel as though we don't have enough information. We tend to assume that other people possess more knowledge of any given situation and that their actions reflect the optimal behaviour.

Why this Principle works:

The principle of Social Proof is driven by our natural desire to behave "correctly": we are social beings, and what other people think is important to us. The pressure to conform is a powerful motivator. The principle also draws from a sense of 'safety in numbers'. Doing the same things as everyone else makes us feel protected and validated in some way. For example, we're more likely to work late if others in our team are doing the same, to put a tip in a jar if it already contains money, or to eat in a restaurant if it's busy. We assume that if others are behaving a certain way then it must be for a reason: the restaurant is good, the service deserves tipping, the work needs to be finished today...

How to use this Principle:

Social Proof also applies to marketing and sales. For example, online marketing strategies such as displaying validation logos, a subscriber count, social shares or testimonials are all based on Social Proof. The amount of followers, views, likes, subscribers or past satisfied customers that a user sees will affect how they perceive the website. It's for this reason that we consult TripAdvisor for hotels and restaurants, Consumer Reports before making purchases, Kayak for flight choices, Yelp for eating out, and so on. We want to check and validate our decisions before we make them to ensure we are making the right choices.

Concrete Application Example:

If you offer your customers the option to sign in using Facebook then make the most of this advantage. Indeed, using Facebook is a good way to quickly access data about a customer, but that's not the only benefit. You can also use it to help persuade them to make a purchase, by displaying those of their Facebook friends who have liked, used, talked about, or purchased the products from your site.

When we are unsure on which decision to make, studies show that we tend to imitate others' behaviour - and nobody will be more persuasive than people we know. We will automatically think that if one of our friends purchased or liked a particular product, then it must be good. The product is given immediate credibility and extra desirability.

Sources and further examples:

Sources:
- Sherif, 1935;
- Asch, 1956

Further examples on this PRIVATE page:
www.smart-persuasion.com/social-proof

Principle 70

Authority Principle

(Milgram, 1960; Cialdini, 1984)

Description of the Principle:

The Authority Principle describes our tendency to obey authority. From a very young age, we are trained to obey people: our parents, teachers, adults, policemen... This obedience isn't necessarily coercive (that is to say, reliant on the use of force) but is more often based on our ingrained reaction to authority figures; there is an unspoken agreement about the balance of control in our societies that is most often adhered to.

Why this Principle works:

There are many elements that can give the impression of authority: expertise, experience, popularity, a uniform (doctor's coat, police uniform...), a title (Dr., Professor, Director...), physical attributes, success or simply an authoritative attitude. Due to the amount of information available, we often use cognitive shortcuts, only relying on one or two attributes linked to authority figures in order to decide whom we should obey. For example, evidence shows that some people only need see a police badge to follow orders, and will not consider whether these orders are legal, or if the police badge is even real.

One of the most famous experiments to demonstrate the Authority Principle is named after the American Psychologist who carried it out: Stanley Milgram. The Milgram experiment aimed to measure the extent to which people will continue to be obedient even when instructed to behave directly against their morality and personal conscience. Participants were paired up, with one becoming the "teacher" and one the "student". This draw was fixed so that the student was always an actor and the teacher was always a real participant. The student had to learn different word pairings and was then attached to a (fake) electro-shock machine. The "teacher" was then instructed to ask the "student" a series of questions about the word pairings and shock them each time they answered incorrectly.

The participants, playing the role of teachers, were accompanied by another actor who was dressed in a recognisably scientific outfit. This actor was placed there as the "authority figure". They continued to encourage participants to give the shocks even when the voltage got higher and "students" began to express pain.

The presence of this legitimised authority, assumed to be competent, meant that very few of the participants questioned the ethics or morality of the orders at all.

A remarkable 62.5% of participants saw the experiment through to the end, giving their partners "shocks" at dangerous levels. The conclusion was that humans will follow orders given by an authority figure, even when those orders should be questioned and disobeyed.

How to use this Principle:

A common application of the Authority Principle is the use of a celebrity endorsement. Sports brands use well-known sports figures to give their products credibility; if a famous footballer says a particular brand of football boots is the best, people will be inclined to believe them.

Another way of making the most of this is by putting expert testimonies or reviews on your website; the knowledge that people of authority from your field endorse your products will make consumers much more likely to want them, too.

Concrete Application Example:

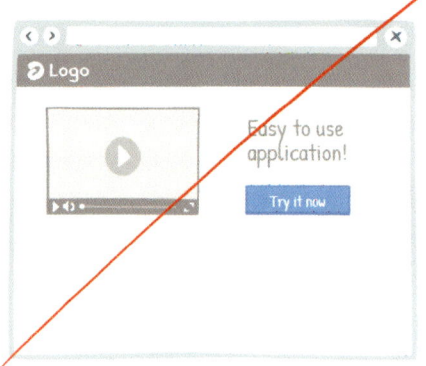 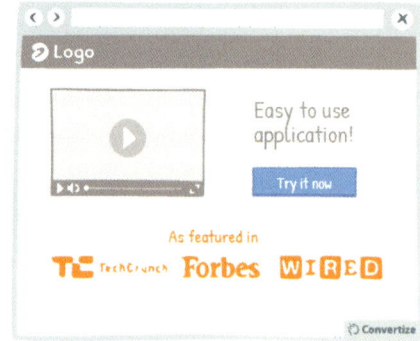

Lending authority to your marketing can be really effective. In today's society people are so bombarded with marketing messages that they don't necessarily place a lot of trust in what they are told.

Adding an element of impartiality and authority to your product or brand with content that shows you are "featured in" or "recommended by" well known authoritative institutions (such as magazines or other respected companies in your field) will lend weight to what you are selling.

It is also proven that we tend to follow the instructions or advice of authority figures, even if we're unsure whether what they are saying is true, as we are socially trained to respect and follow authority without asking questions.

Sources and further examples:

Sources:
- Milgram, 1960
- Cialdini, 1984

Further examples on this PRIVATE page:
www.smart-persuasion.com/authority-principle

Social Comparison Theory

Principle 71

(Festinger, 1954; Thorton & Arrowood, 1966)

Description of the Principle:

Social Comparison Theory, first described by social psychologist Leo Festinger in 1954, is centred on the fact that individuals have an intrinsic drive to evaluate themselves and that they prefer to do this through direct comparison with others. Humans are not satisfied with absolute merits and so make use of social comparison to reduce uncertainty and access a more trusted way to define the self.

Why this Principle works:

For Social Comparison and self-evaluation, people tend to select someone reasonably similar to themselves. For example, when evaluating how successful a career has been so far, individuals are more likely to compare themselves to someone who is from a similar background with comparable education and social experiences. This provides a more accurate idea of how successful they have been. Consumers are also likely to compare their shopping experiences to that of others who are making the same or similar purchases. No one wants to feel as though they are missing out on a deal or paying a higher price for the same thing. Whether the price offered is fair or not is of little consequence; people will decide whether it is fair for them dependent on whether they perceive other consumers to be getting a better deal.

How to use this Principle:

When shopping online, people will be put off making the final purchase if it is apparent that others might receive a discount. For example, if there is an "enter your discount code here" box on the final purchase page, or if it is clearly stated that "Members should enter their membership number to get free delivery", those without access to these deals might choose not to complete their purchase.

This situation can be avoided in two ways to help optimise conversions: either make the discount option less prominent or replace an open box with a question such as "Do you have a discount code?" to take away the feeling of being part of the group who have to pay full price for something. This should increase the likelihood of a conversion. However, if members do receive a discount, making this fact prominent and including a 'Sign up!' Call To Action could increase these conversions.

Concrete Application Example:

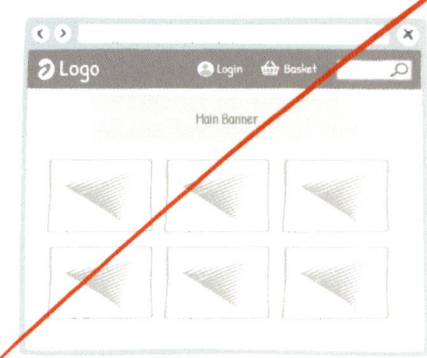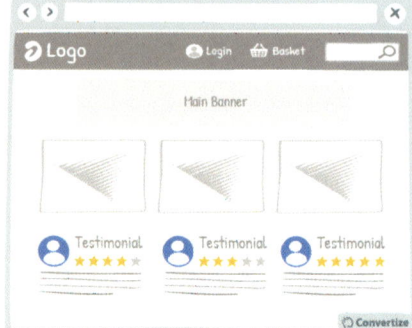

If you have positive reviews about your products or services, then display them on your homepage. Encouraging potential customers to compare themselves to previous customers can be an effective persuasion technique. The more similar the featured reviewers are to your target market, the more effective this technique will be.

Sources and further examples:

Sources:
- Festinger, 1954
- Thorton & Arrowood, 1966

Further examples on this PRIVATE page:
www.smart-persuasion.com/social-comparison-theory

Principle 72

Social Cognition

(Pelham, Carvallo & Jones, 2003)

Description of the Principle:

This principle, studied by Pelham, Carvallo and Jones (2003) asserts that people gravitate toward people, places, and things that resemble themselves. It is an unconscious process that is grounded in people's favourable self-associations: they are biased towards characteristics that relate to themselves. In other words, people like something they have a connection with, even though they may not be aware that this is the reason they feel favourably towards it. For example, customers will gravitate towards a business or website that they feel they share something in common with or that relates directly to them. This principle of Social Cognition is also referred to as Implicit Egotism.

Why this Principle works:

Academic research has shown through several studies that people's personal details are likely to affect their life choices. For instance, there are statistically more people named Louis living in the city of St. Louis than in any other city, and people named Dennis or Denise become dentists more often than people with other names. It has also been shown that there is a direct correlation between people's birthdays and the number of their address. It seems that people subconsciously choose towns, careers and addresses that have a link with the primary elements of their identity (name, age, birthday, etc.).

How to use this Principle:

This cognitive bias has numerous applications in marketing and sales. It is good practice for brands to adapt their marketing strategies to their target audience in order to incite an immediate sense of familiarity and connection to the product, even perhaps including the customer's specific details within their product where possible. For example, brands such as Starbucks Coffee and Coca-Cola put the names of their customers on their coffee cups and Coca-Cola bottles, immediately making them feel more connected with the brand.

Concrete Application Example:

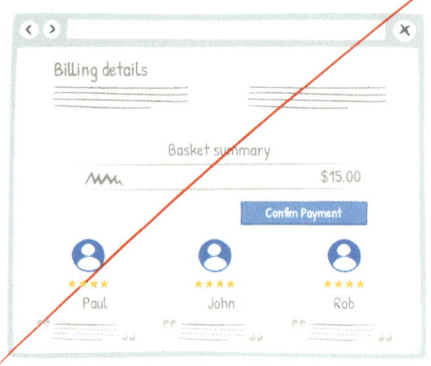 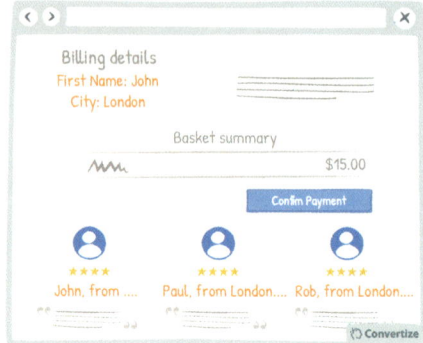

Implicit Egotism, a common effect within Social Cognition, can be used strategically when displaying information about your previous customers. For example, you can improve the persuasiveness of your checkout page by showing targeted testimonials. By the time a customer arrives at your checkout page, they have already given you their name and address. Geolocation data is also available for every browser who visits your site. So, instead of displaying the same content every time, your page should provide testimonials that are specific to your current visitor's name, location or the town they live in. If your database of testimonials is not large enough to provide targeted content for your checkout page, you can simply personalise the text. Add a line saying: "X customers from Y have also bought this item," or "Deliveries to Y typically take X days." People gravitate around information that relates to them personally. Using specific names or locations improves Cognitive Ease (Principal 23) and reduces the likelihood that they will abandon your checkout.

Sources and further examples:

Sources:
- Sherif, 1935; Asch, 1956
- Pelham, Carvallo & Jones, 2003

Further examples on this PRIVATE page:
www.smart-persuasion.com/social-cognition

Conclusion

Cognitive biases can make a real impact—on human interactions, on your marketing, and in the world at large.

On October 9, 2017, Richard Thaler was awarded the Nobel Prize for his work on behavioural economics. Thaler, a professor at the University of Chicago Booth School of Business, is considered to be one of the founders of his field. His best-selling book, *Nudge*, established the concept of "nudging", in which indirect persuasion is used to influence the behaviour and decisions of large groups of people. For example, in his book, Thaler discusses the conundrum of a school that wanted its students to make healthier choices in the cafeteria. Campaigns and subsidies were not working. However, simply placing healthier choices like fruits and vegetables at eye level led to an enormous spike in healthier decisions at lunchtime.

Following the award of the Nobel Prize to Richard Thaler, David Halpern (Chief Executive of the UK Government's Behavioural Insights Team) wrote an article for *The Guardian* about the impact of Nudge Theory. The Behavioural Insights Team works alongside the government to determine how small changes in policy can produce big impacts on public behaviour.

For example, Halpern's research found that changing the wording in recruitment emails for police departments in Avon and Somerset increased the number of BAME candidates who applied by 50%. This minor change in wording significantly improved police diversity. In another case, sending taxpayers reminders to submit their payments was found to produce a £30 million increase in tax payments, particularly when the letters noted that the money would go to fund the NHS and other social services. Similarly, weekly text messages sent to students enrolled in adult literacy classes reduced dropout rates by 36%.

Halpern's successful use of Thaler's Nudge Theory shows that cognitive biases, the psychological "shortcuts" that allow us to process information more easily, can have profound and far-reaching impacts on our behaviour.

Changing the colour of your CTAs, adjusting the gaze direction of your models, and adding testimonials to your website are reliable tactics for increasing conversions. Even so, it is still important to remember what people like Halpern and Thaler do with thier ideas: test them. Halpern suggests that 2 out of every 10 exeriments of his fail. Thaler himself came to psychology while struggling with his economics doctorate. He could not explain why the people he was studying did not act as classical economics suggested they would. It was because of this obstacle that he was advised to study the work of Daniel Kahneman and Amos Tversky, prompting the start of a new era of behavioural economics.

Cognitive biases can help you to persuade your website visitors to become customers, but there is still a lot of hard work that must be done. Copywriting, marketing campaigns, and clever website design are just a few of the elements that are necessary for these persuasive techniques to work as successfully as possible.

If you are trying to encourage people to eat more healthily, you need to have the apples and oranges available to give them. You also need the shelves to put them on and the signs to point them out. Only when these things are in place can you start to make the display more persuasive. As an e-commerce marketer seeking to guide your customers' behaviour, learning about cognitive biases and persuasive techniques won't do any good without the products, user experience and marketing that your customers expect. However, by combining these elements with persuasive strategies, you will achieve results you never thought possible.

So, take it from the Nobel Prize committee, a century of social and psychological researchers, and from all of us here at Convertize: cognitive biases matter. Whilst marketing trends come and go, our brains are here to stay. Let's talk to them in a language they understand.

Happy optimising!

- **Jochen & Philippe**

Resources

- https://www.theguardian.com/commentisfree/2017/oct/10/behavioural-economics-richard-thaler-nudge-nobel-prize-winner
- https://www.theguardian.com/public-leaders-network/2015/jul/23/rise-nudge-unit-politicians-human-behaviour
- https://www.theguardian.com/books/2015/jul/04/misbehaving-making-behavioural-economics-richard-h-thaler-review-nudge
- http://www.bbc.co.uk/news/business-41549753

Printed in Great Britain
by Amazon